Grammar is a puzzle; each word helps create a beautiful picture.

Be a grammar chef: mix nouns, verbs, and adjectives to cook up tasty sentences!

YOUR NAME:

Welcome to 10th Grade English Grammar! We want to ensure that this year is both challenging and rewarding for you. To help us understand your needs and areas of interest, please answer the following questions:

1. **Name/School (Optional):** _____

2. **Previous Experience:**
   - How confident do you feel about your current understanding of English grammar? (Scale 1-5, 1 being not confident at all and 5 being very confident)
   - [ ] 1 [ ] 2 [ ] 3 [ ] 4 [ ] 5

3. **Areas of Struggle:**
   - Are there specific grammar topics you find challenging? Please list them below or mark any that apply:
   - [ ] Sentence Structure (simple, compound, complex)
   - [ ] Punctuation (commas, semicolons, etc.)
   - [ ] Parts of Speech (nouns, verbs, adjectives, etc.)
   - [ ] Verb Tenses
   - [ ] Subject-Verb Agreement
   - [ ] Passive vs. Active Voice
   - [ ] Other: _____

4. **Learning Preferences:**
   - How do you prefer to learn new grammar concepts? (Choose any that apply)
   - [ ] Visual aids (charts, diagrams)
   - [ ] Interactive activities (group work, games)
   - [ ] Written explanations and examples
   - [ ] Video tutorials
   - [ ] Other: _____

5. **Past Feedback:**
   - Have you received specific feedback on your grammar in the past that you'd like to address? Please describe briefly:
   - _____

6. **Goals:**
   - What are your personal goals for improving your grammar this year?
   - _____

7. **Reading and Writing:**
   - Do you feel that your reading and writing skills impact your understanding of grammar? If yes, how so?
   - _____

8. **Feedback Frequency:**
   - How often would you like to receive feedback on your grammar exercises?
   - [ ] After every exercise
   - [ ] Weekly
   - [ ] Bi-weekly
   - [ ] Monthly

9. **Additional Support:**
   - Are there any additional supports or resources that you think would help you learn grammar better?
   - _____

10. **Additional Comments:**
    - Please feel free to add any other comments or concerns you have regarding grammar learning:
    - _____

Exploring the Nuances of Advanced Parts of Speech

Understanding the subtleties of parts of speech is crucial for mastering English language nuances. This worksheet delves into more complex aspects, focusing on various types of pronouns, verbs, and adverbs.

Pronouns:

Relative Pronouns: Used to link a clause to a noun or pronoun. Common examples include 'who,' 'whom,' 'whose,' 'which,' and 'that.'

Demonstrative Pronouns: Point to and identify a noun or a pronoun. 'This,' 'that,' 'these,' and 'those' are demonstrative pronouns.

Indefinite Pronouns: Refer to nonspecific things or people. Examples include 'someone,' 'anything,' 'everyone,' and 'few.'

Verbs:

Modal Verbs: Express necessity, possibility, permission, or ability. Common modal verbs are 'can,' 'could,' 'may,' 'might,' 'must,' 'shall,' 'should,' 'will,' and 'would.'

Phrasal Verbs: Combinations of a verb with one or more prepositions or adverbs, which then create a meaning different from the original verb. Examples are 'give up,' 'look after,' and 'break down.'

Adverbs:

Frequency Adverbs: Describe how often something occurs. Examples include 'always,' 'usually,' 'often,' 'sometimes,' and 'never.'

Manner Adverbs: Describe how something is done. Common examples are 'slowly,' 'quickly,' 'carefully,' and 'easily.'

Degree Adverbs: Modify adjectives or other adverbs, indicating the level or intensity. Examples are 'very,' 'quite,' 'almost,' and 'too.'

Multiple Choice Questions

Which relative pronoun is correctly used to refer to people?
a) Which b) That c) Who d) Whose

Identify the modal verb in the following sentence: "She might go to the concert tonight."
a) She b) Go c) Might d) Concert

True or False

'Regularly' is an example of a frequency adverb.

True

False

All phrasal verbs consist of a verb and a preposition.

True

False

Short Answer Questions

Create a sentence using 'nevertheless' as an adverb of degree.

_____

Give an example of a sentence using 'underneath' as a demonstrative pronoun.

_____

Here's a reminder of the main parts of speech along with some basic rules for you to study:

1. Nouns: Words that name people, places, things, or ideas.
   - **Rule**: Nouns can be singular or plural, and they can be the subject or object in a sentence.
   - Example: "Dog", "city", "happiness".

2. Pronouns: Words that take the place of nouns.
   - **Rule**: Pronouns must agree in number (singular or plural) and gender with the nouns they replace.
   - Example: "he", "they", "it".

3. Verbs: Words that express actions or states of being.
   - **Rule**: Verbs must agree with the subject in number and tense.
   - Example: "run", "is", "were".

4. Adjectives: Words that describe or modify nouns or pronouns.
   - **Rule**: Adjectives can come before a noun or after a linking verb.
   - Example: "blue", "happy", "tall".

5. Adverbs: Words that modify verbs, adjectives, or other adverbs.
   - **Rule**: Adverbs often end in "-ly" and can express manner, place, time, or degree.
   - Example: "quickly", "there", "very".

6. Prepositions: Words that show the relationship between a noun or pronoun and other words in a sentence.
   - **Rule**: Prepositions are usually followed by a noun or pronoun.
   - Example: "in", "on", "at".

7. **Conjunctions**: Words that join words, phrases, or clauses.
   - **Rule**: Conjunctions coordinate words or groups of words of equal grammatical structure.
   - Example: "and", "but", "or".

8. **Interjections**: Words that express emotion or a sudden sentiment.
   - **Rule**: Interjections are often followed by an exclamation point and can stand alone.
   - Example: "Wow!", "Oh!", "Hey!"

Prepositions of Place and Direction

Score: _____

Date: _____

Prepositions are words that indicate relationships between other words in a sentence. Prepositions of place and direction are particularly important as they help to specify where something is or the direction in which something is moving. Common prepositions of place include 'on,' 'in,' 'under,' 'next to,' 'between,' etc., while prepositions of direction include 'to,' 'toward,' 'into,' 'out of,' 'through,' etc.

Multiple Choice Questions

Which preposition is commonly used to indicate that something is inside a container or an enclosed space? a) On b) Above c) In d) Under

Choose the correct preposition of direction in the following sentence: "She walked ___ the store." a) into b) on c) above d) beside

True or False

'Above' is a preposition of place that indicates a higher level than something else.

- True
- False

The preposition 'through' cannot be used to indicate direction.

- True
- False

Short Answer Questions

Create a sentence using 'between' as a preposition of place.

....

....

Explain the difference between 'into' and 'onto' as prepositions of direction.

....

....

Advanced Punctuations

Colon (:): Used to introduce a list, a quote, an explanation, or a consequence. It often comes after a complete sentence and introduces something related to that sentence.

Semicolon (;): Links two independent clauses that are closely related in thought. It can also be used in lists where items contain commas.

Dash (—): Used to create a strong break in the structure of a sentence. It can add emphasis, introduce an explanation, or replace other punctuation like colons or semicolons.

Hyphen (-): Used to join words in a compound term, or to show a break in a word at the end of a line.

1. **Multiple Choice:** Which sentence correctly uses a colon?

   A) She has one goal: to find the treasure.

   B) She has one goal, to find: the treasure.

2. **True or False:** A semicolon is correctly used in the following sentence: "He loves hiking; his brother prefers fishing."

3. **Short Answer:** Rewrite this sentence using a dash: "I have everything I need for the trip, including a compass, a map, and a flashlight."

---

4. **Multiple Choice:** Where should a hyphen be used?

 (A) Twenty four hours. (B) Twenty-four hours   (C) Twenty - four hours

5. **True or False:** A colon can be used to introduce a quotation.

6. **Fill in the Blank:** Use a semicolon in the blank: "Lisa loves to read _____ her sister enjoys writing."

7. **Multiple Choice:** Choose the sentence where the dash is used correctly.

   A) I need to buy eggs, milk, bread — and don't forget cheese.

   B) I need to buy eggs — milk, bread, and don't forget cheese.

   C) I need to buy — eggs, milk, bread, and don't forget cheese.

8. **True or False:** A hyphen is used to connect two related words into a compound adjective.

9. **Short Answer:** Insert a colon correctly in this sentence: "She knew what her choice would be pizza."

---

10. **Fill in the Blank:** Complete the sentence with a dash or a hyphen: "This is a well___known author."

Complex Sentence Structures

Complex sentences are fundamental in English, providing depth and detail. They consist of one independent clause and at least one dependent clause, connected by subordinating conjunctions, relative clauses, and various conjunction types.

1. **Subordinate Clauses:** A subordinate clause (or dependent clause) does not express a complete thought and cannot stand alone. It is usually introduced by a subordinating conjunction like 'although,' 'because,' 'since,' or 'after.'

2. **Relative Clauses:** These provide additional information about a noun or pronoun in a sentence. They begin with relative pronouns such as 'who,' 'whom,' 'whose,' 'which,' or 'that.'

3. **Types of Conjunctions:**

   - **Coordinating Conjunctions:** Connect clauses of equal importance (e.g., 'and,' 'but,' 'or').

   - **Subordinating Conjunctions:** Link a dependent clause to an independent clause (e.g., 'although,' 'since').

   - **Correlative Conjunctions:** Work in pairs to join clauses or phrases (e.g., 'neither...nor,' 'either...or').

Multiple Choice Questions

1. Which of the following is a subordinating conjunction?

(a) And (b) Although (c) Or (d) Both

2. Choose the sentence that correctly uses a relative clause.

   a) She went to the store, and she bought some apples.

   b) The book that I read was fascinating.

   c) I enjoy running but not swimming.

   d) Either you start now, or you'll be late.

True or False

3. A complex sentence must contain at least two independent clauses.

   - True or - False

4. 'Where' and 'when' can be used as relative pronouns in a relative clause.

   - True or - False

Short Answer Questions

5. Create a complex sentence using 'unless' as a subordinating conjunction.

Compound and Complex Sentences

In the kingdom of Grammar, two royal siblings lived: Compound and Complex Sentence. They were known for their distinct ways of speaking.

Compound Sentence: the elder of the two loved to share two equally important ideas. He was like a train with two connected carriages, each carrying a complete thought. He used coordinating conjunctions such as 'and,' 'but,' or 'so' to connect his ideas.

For example, Compound would say, "I love reading books, and I also enjoy playing football." Here, both 'I love reading books' and 'I also enjoy playing football' are complete thoughts connected by 'and.'

Complex Sentence: the younger sibling liked to share one main idea and an additional detail. He was like a tree with a large trunk (main idea) and a smaller branch (additional detail). He used subordinating conjunctions such as 'because,' 'since,' or 'although' to connect his ideas.

For instance, Complex would say, "Although it was raining, I went for a walk." Here, 'I went for a walk' is the main idea, and 'Although it was raining' is the additional detail connected by 'although.'

Activity:

Now, imagine you're invited to a royal ball in the kingdom of Grammar. You'll be meeting Compound and Complex Sentence. What would you say to them?

1. Write two sentences you would say to Compound Sentence, using 'and,' 'but,' or 'so' to connect your ideas. Remember, both your ideas should be equally important.

2. Write two sentences you would say to Complex Sentence, using 'because,' 'since,' or 'although' to connect your ideas. Remember, one idea should be more important than the other.

Remember, in the kingdom of Grammar, creativity is your crown. So, let your imagination rule and have fun with your sentences!

Use this section below to complete your Activity & any Extra Credit work

Abbreviations

An abbreviation is a word that has been shortened. When writing, abbreviations can make it easier and faster to say what you need to say.

There are numerous kinds of abbreviations that can be used. Let us now go over some of the most common ones.

Months

Except for March, April, May, June, and July, the majority of the months are long words. When writing long ones, you might want to use an abbreviation. For example, if you're writing a sticky note to remind a friend to meet you at the ice cream shop at 1:00 p.m. on August 6, you can use the abbreviation 'Aug.' Except for the short months, such as 'May,' each month has an abbreviation.

Because the months of the year begin with capital letters, the abbreviations should, too. Each abbreviation should be followed by a period. What is the abbreviation for the month in which Christmas falls? Dec. Correct! What about this Halloween? Oct. is correct!

Week Days
The words for the days of the week are also quite long! The abbreviations are as follows:

- Mon. – Monday
- Tues. or Tue. – Tuesday
- Wed. – Wednesday
- Thu. or Thurs. – Thursday
- Fri. – Friday
- Sat.- Saturday
- Sun. – Sunday

Addresses

When sending letters or packages via mail, you must include an address. You can use abbreviations in the address so that the true word takes up less space, and an abbreviation is faster.

If you're sending a birthday card to Aunt Kay, who lives on 31st Avenue, you can simply write '31st Ave.' If you want to send a friendly note to your favorite teacher who lives on Rose Street, use the abbreviation 'Rose St.' If you want to send a thank-you note to your best friend who lives in an apartment, write 'Apt. #2' rather than Apartment #2. You can also substitute 'Dr.' for Drive and 'Blvd.' for Boulevard. See? When writing addresses, abbreviations come in handy!

- N- North
- E- East
- S- South
- W- West
- bldg.- building
- st.- Street

States

Finally, when writing the names of states, you can use abbreviations. When mailing something to someone, the most common place to abbreviate a state is on an envelope.

For example, the abbreviation for Virginia is 'VA.' The United States Postal Service assigns an abbreviation to each state so that everyone uses the same abbreviations when mailing a letter or a package.

Instructions: Match the abbreviation to the correct word.

1		Ave.	northeast	A
2		Blvd.	southeast	B
3		Dr.	Boulevard	C
4		Ln.	east	D
5		Rd.	south	E
6		St.	miscellaneous	F
7		E	Mistress	G
8		N	Street	H
9		NE	department	I
10		NW	west	J
11		S	estimated time of arrival	K
12		SE	Road	L
13		SW	north	M
14		W	Mister	N
15		dept.	Avenue	O
16		D.I.Y.	minute or minimum	P
17		est.	Do it yourself	Q
18		E.T.A.	Drive	R
19		min.	established	S
20		misc.	Lane	T
21		Mr.	northwest	U
22		Mrs.	southwest	V

Prefixes

A prefix is a part of a word or a word contained within another word. It is added to the beginning of another word to give it a new meaning. Additionally, it can refer to a number that is added at the beginning to indicate the position of anything inside a group.

Rules for adding prefix:

- prefix + root word = new word.

Look at the meaning of the prefix added to the meaning of the root word to get the meaning of the new word.

Meanings for prefixes vary depending on which one is used.

Example:

anti- | opposing, against, the opposite| antibiotic

com- | with, jointly, completely | combat

de- | down, away| decrease|

extra- | outside, beyond | extracurricular

1. **A prefix comes at the _____ of a word.**
   a. beginning
   b. end

2. **A prefix changes the meaning of a root word.**
   a. True
   b. False

3. **What do you think the prefix re- (redo) means _____?**
   a. do again
   b. not - or - opposite

4. **What do you think the prefix dis- (disadvantage) means _____?**
   a. add; multiply
   b. away; removal

5. **If you are unable to do something, you are _____.**
   a. able to do it again
   b. not able to do it

6. **If you dislike green beans, you _____.**
   a. really like green beans
   b. do not like green beans

7. **If you disobey your parents, you _____.**
   a. obey your parents quickly
   b. do not obey your parents

8. **My teacher made me ___write name because it was sloppy.**
   a. un
   b. re

9. **My friends and I __play our favorite video games over and over again.**
   a. re
   b. dis

10. **Kids are __able to drive until they are 16.**
    a. un
    b. re

Suffix

A suffix is a letter or group of letters attached to the end of a word in order to alter the meaning or function of the word. As with prefixes, the English language comes with tons of suffixes.

Consider the suffix **-ist**; by adding it to a word, you can modify it to refer to someone who performs or practices something. So, **art** becomes **artist**, a skillful performer of a particular art.

Other Examples:

The suffix **-ish** (Blueish) means relating to or resembling something.

The suffix **-ness** (Happiness) indicates a condition or quality. This suffix changes the word from a verb to a noun.

The suffix **-ship** (internship) position held.

The suffix **-less** (restless) means without something.

1. What is a suffix?
    a. A word beginning that changes the meaning of the word
    b. A word ending that changes the meaning of the word

2. What is the suffix in the word "permission"?
    a. -per
    b. -sion

3. What is the suffix in the word careful?
    a. -care
    b. -ful

4. What is the suffix in the word youngest?
    a. -young
    b. -est

5. What is the suffix in the word harmless?
    a. -less
    b. -arm

6. What is the suffix in the word cuter?
    a. -cute
    b. -er

7. What do you think the suffix -less means?
    a. Meaning: More of
    b. Meaning: Without

8. What do you think the suffix -ward, -wards means? (Towards, afterwards, backwards, inward)
    a. Meaning: Direction
    b. Meaning: Driving something

9. What do you think the suffix -ery means? (bakery, pottery, nursery)
    a. Meaning: an occupation or a way to make a living
    b. Meaning: a business or trade, a behavior, a condition

10. What is the suffix in the word breakable?
    a. -able
    b. -break

Homophones vs Homographs
vs. Homonyms

How do you know which 'there,' 'their,' or 'they're' to use when you're writing? Isn't it a difficult one? These words sound similar but have completely different meanings.

Words with the same sound but different meanings are referred to as **homophones**. Homophones can be spelled differently or the same way. Rose (the flower), rose (the past tense of 'rise,' and rows (a line of items or people) are all homophones.

Homographs are two or more words that have the same spelling but different meanings and it **doesn't have to sound the same**. Because homographs are words with multiple meanings, how can you tell which one is being used? Readers can determine which form of a homograph is being used by looking for context clues, or words surrounding it that provide information about the definition. Take a look at these homograph examples.

A **bat** is either a piece of sporting equipment or an animal.
Bass is either a type of fish or a musical genre.
A **pen** is a writing instrument or a small enclosure in which animals are kept.
Lean is a word that means to be thin or to rest against something.
A **skip** is a fictitious jump or missing out on something.

Homonyms are words that have the same spelling or pronunciation but different meanings. These words can be perplexing at times, especially for students learning to spell them. For example, right means moral, the opposite of left, and a personal freedom. Homonyms can refer to both homophones and homographs. Both a homograph and a homophone are included in the definition of a homonym. For example, the words 'bear,' 'tear,' and 'lead' are all homographs, but they also meet the criteria for homonyms. They simply have to have the same look or sound. Similarly, while the words 'sell,' 'cell,' 'by,' and 'buy' are all homophones, they are also homonyms.

1. 'there,' 'their,' or 'they're' are examples of _____.
   a. Homophones
   b. Homographs

2. _____ are words that have the same spelling or pronunciation but different meanings.
   a. Homonyms
   b. Hemograms

3. Choose the correct homophone for this sentence: Please don't drop and _____that bottle of hand sanitizer!
   a. brake
   b. break

4. Homographs are two or more words that have the same spelling but different _____.
   a. ending sounds
   b. meanings

5. Current (A flow of water / Up to date) is both homograph and homophone.
   a. True
   b. False

6. To, two, and too are _____.
   a. Homonyms
   b. Homagraphs

7. The candle filled the _____ with a delicious scent.
   a. air
   b. heir

8. Kim drove _____ the tunnel.
   a. threw
   b. through

9. **John wants to go to _____ house for dinner, but they don't like her, so _____ going to say no.**

    a. there, they're

    b. their, they're

10. **We won a $95,000 _____!**

    a. check

    b. cheque

11. **For example, a pencil is not really made with _____.**

    a. led

    b. lead

12. **Choose the correct homophone for this sentence: Timmy was standing _____ in line.**

    a. fourth

    b. forth

13. **Homophones are two words that sound the same but have a different meanings.**

    a. True

    b. False

14. **The word ring in the following two sentences is considered what? She wore a ruby <u>ring</u>. | We heard the doorbell <u>ring</u>.**

    a. hologram

    b. homograph

15. **A Homograph is a word that has more than one meaning and doesn't have to sound the same.**

    a. True

    b. False

16. **Homophones occur when there are multiple ways to spell the same sound.**

    a. True

    b. False

17. **Select the correct homophone: I have very little (patience/patients) when students do not follow directions.**

    a. patience

    b. patients

18. **The correct homophone (s) are used in the sentence: Personally, I hate the smell of read meet.**

    a. True

    b. False

19. **The correct homophone(s) is used in the sentence: We saw a herd of cattle in the farmer's field.**

    a. True

    b. False

20. **What is NOT an example of a homograph?**

    a. or, oar

    b. live, live

21. **I love my _____ class.**

    a. dear

    b. deer

22. **We will go _____ after we finish our lesson.**

    a. there

    b. their

23. **Please grab _____ jacket for recess.**

    a. you're

    b. your

24. **There is _____ more water at the concession stand.**

    a. no

    b. know

Collective Noun

A collective noun is a noun that refers to a group of people, animals, or things. They are described as a single entity. Collective nouns are distinct from singular nouns in that singular nouns describe only one person or object.

Many collective nouns are common nouns, but when they are the name of a company or other organization with more than one person, such as Microsoft, they can also be proper nouns.

Find the collective noun in each sentence.

1. Our class visited the natural history museum on a field trip.

2. The bison herd stampeded across the prairie, leaving a massive dust cloud in its wake.

3. We eagerly awaited the verdict of the jury.

4. This year's basketball team features three players who stand taller than six feet.

5. At Waterloo, Napoleon's army was finally defeated.

6. The plans for a new park have been approved by the town council.

7. He comes from a large family, as the oldest of eleven children.

8. The rock group has been on tour for several months.

9. When Elvis appeared on stage, the entire audience erupted in applause.

10. The San Francisco crowd were their usual individualistic selves.

11. The crew of sailors boarded the ships.

12. A mob destroyed the company's new office.

13. The fleet of ships was waiting at the port.

14. It was difficult for the committee to come to a decision.

Concrete & Abstract Noun

In the English language, both concrete and abstract nouns are essential parts of speech. The primary distinction between concrete and abstract nouns is that concrete nouns refer to people, places, or things that take up physical space, whereas abstract nouns refer to intangible ideas that cannot be physically interacted with.

Words like "luck," "disgust," and "empathy" are examples of abstract nouns. While it is possible to see someone being empathetic, empathy is not a visible or tangible entity. The majority of feelings, emotions, and philosophies can be classified as abstract nouns.

1. FIND THE ABSTRACT NOUN ?
   a. KIND
   b. BOOK

2. FIND THE CONCRETE NOUNS
   a. WINDOW
   b. LOVE

3. FIND THE ABSTRACT NOUN: THE KING WAS KNOWN FOR HIS JUSTICE
   a. JUSTICE
   b. KING

4. WHAT ARE THE 5 CONCRETE NOUNS
   a. TASTE, SMELL, WALKING, EYEING, TOUCHING
   b. SMELL,TASTE, SIGHT, HEARING,TOUCH

5. WHICH NOUN BELOW IS AN ABSTRACT NOUN?
   a. TRAIN
   b. LOVE

6. IS THE FOLLOWING NOUN CONCRETE OR ABSTRACT? CUPCAKES
   a. ABSTRACT
   b. CONCRETE

7. WHAT IS A CONCRETE NOUN?
   a. A NOUN THAT YOU CAN EXPERIENCE WITH AT LEAST 1 OF YOUR 5 SENSES.
   b. A NOUN THAT YOU CAN'T EXPERIENCE WITH AT LEAST 1 OF YOUR 5 SENSES.

8. WHICH WORD BELOW IS AN ABSTRACT NOUN?
   a. BRAVERY
   b. FRIEND

9. WHICH WORD BELOW IS NOT A CONCRETE NOUN?
   a. HAMBURGER
   b. ANGER

10. IS THE WORD THOUGHTFULNESS A CONCRETE OR ABSTRACT NOUN?
   a. ABSTRACT
   b. CONCRETE

Capitalization Rules Refresher

1. What are the most common pronouns?

2. What is a proper noun?

3. Do common nouns name specific persons, places, things, or ideas?

4. Always capitalize the first letter in the first word of a sentence?

5. Always capitalize the first letter in the first word in a quotation?

6. Always capitalize the first letter in the first word of a greeting or closing?

7. Always capitalize the first letter in the first and last name of a person?

8. Never capitalize the pronoun "I"?

9. Always capitalize the first letter in the names of: streets, roads, cities, and states?

10. Always capitalize the first letter in each part of the name of a specific building or monument: Statue of Liberty, Empire State Building, Pensacola Chamber of Commerce . . .?

11. Always capitalize the titles of: video games, stories, movies, and TV shows

12. Always capitalize the days of the weeks?

13. The names of months should not be capitalized?

14. Always capitalize major holidays except christmas and thanksgiving?

Preposition

Prepositional phrases are collections of words that contain prepositions. Remember that prepositions are words that indicate the relationships between different elements in a sentence, and you'll have no trouble identifying prepositional phrases.

Another way to look at it, a prepositional phrase is a group of words that function as a unified part of speech despite the absence of a verb or a subject. It is usually made up of a preposition and a noun or a preposition and a pronoun.

Under the rock is an example of a prepositional phrase. In this example, the preposition is "under," and the prepositional phrase is "under the rock."

Choose the correct preposition.

up	up	off	out	through
down	on	away	together	off
about	out	upon	off	across

1. He pulled _____ his cancer treatment very well.

2. We must pull _____ to make this work.

3. Why don't you put ____ the yellow dress?

4. I have put _____ my holidays until later this year.

5. I don't know how she puts ____ with noisy children all day.

6. The CFS put _____ six fires today.

7. I feel quite run _____ since I got my cold.

8. I might go to Hobart to run _____ from this heat.

9. Coles has run _____ of bread today.

10. You need to set _____ writing your resume.

11. You will never guess who I ran _____ today!

12. I will go to the airport to see _____ my best friend.

13. He set _____ for Paris last Saturday.

14. The little dog was set _____ by a big dog.

15. Many students want to set ____ their own business.

Acronym

Name: _____

Date: _____

A common way to make an acronym is to use the first letter of each word in a phrase to make a word that can be spoken. This is a great way to make a longer, more complicated phrase easier to say and shorter.

Carefully choose the acronym for each word or phrase.

1. Also Known As
   a. AKA
   b. KAA

2. Central Standard Time
   a. CST
   b. TCS

3. Doing Business As
   a. DBA
   b. ASDOING

4. Do Not Disturb
   a. NOTDN
   b. DND

5. Electronic Data Systems
   a. SDE
   b. EDS

6. End of Day
   a. EOD
   b. ENDDAY

7. Eastern Standard Time
   a. EST
   b. TSE

8. Estimated Time of Arrival
   a. ET
   b. ETA

9. Human Resources
   a. HRS
   b. HR

10. Masters of Business Administration
   a. MOBA
   b. MBA

11. MST - Mountain Standard Time
   a. MST
   b. MSTS

12. Overtime
   a. OTIME
   b. OT

13. Point Of Service
   a. POS
   b. POOS

14. Pacific Standard Time
   a. PST
   b. PSTE

15. Anti-lock Braking System
   a. LOCKBS
   b. ABS

16. Attention Deficit Disorder
   a. ADD
   b. ATTDD

17. Attention Deficit Hyperactivity Disorder
    a. ADHP
    b. ADHD

18. Acquired Immune Deficiency Syndrome
    a. ACQIMDEF
    b. AIDS

19. Centers for Disease Control and Prevention
    a. CDC
    b. CDCP

20. Dead On Arrival
    a. DONA
    b. DOA

21. Date Of Birth
    a. DOB
    b. DOFB

22. Do It Yourself
    a. DIY
    b. DIYO

23. Frequently Asked Questions
    a. FAQA
    b. FAQ

24. Graphics Interchange Format
    a. GIF
    b. GIFF

25. Human Immunodeficiency Virus
    a. HIV
    b. HIMMV

26. Medical Doctor
    a. MD
    b. MED

27. Over The Counter
    a. OTC
    b. OTHEC

28. Pay Per View
    a. PPV
    b. PAYPPV

29. Sound Navigation And Ranging
    a. SONAR
    b. SONAVR

30. Sports Utility Vehicle
    a. SPOUV
    b. SUV

Adjectives to Describe People

Adjectives are descriptive or modifying words for nouns or pronouns. For instance, adjectives such as red, quick, happy, and annoying exist to describe things—a red hat, a speedy rabbit, a cheerful duck, and an obnoxious individual.

Unscramble the adjectives to describe people.

polite	friendly	clever	outgoing	good looking	handsome
cute	fat	tall	smart	young	pretty
attractive	rude	easygoing	funny	confident	tidy
old	beautiful	generous	ugly		

1. ulbuefita   _ e _ _ t _ _ _ _

2. trpyet   _ _ _ _ t y

3. etuc   _ u _ _

4. luyg   _ g _ _

5. ugnyo   _ _ u _ _

6. tleipo   _ _ _ i t _

7. nnufy   f _ _ _ _

8. riledfny   _ _ _ _ n d _ _

9. ohemndsa   _ a _ _ _ o _ _

10. rdue   _ u _ _

11. dol   o _ _

12. aft   _ _ t

13. mrtas   _ _ _ r _

14. idty   _ i _ _

15. yogsgeain   _ _ s _ g _ _ _ _

16. cleerv   c _ e _ _ _

17. neeugrso   g _ n _ _ _ _ _

18. fnitnedoc   _ _ n f _ _ _ _ _

19. tngioogu   o _ _ g _ _ _ _

20. dgoo oinogkl   _ _ _ _ _ o _ _ _ n _

21. vractatite   a _ _ _ a _ _ _ e

22. tlla   t _ _ _

Contractions Multiple Choice

A *contraction* is a way of making two words into one. Circle the correct answer.

1. aren't
  a. are not
  b. not are
  c. arenot

2. can't
  a. cants
  b. cannot
  c. cant

3. couldn't
  a. couldnt
  b. couldnts
  c. could not

4. didn't
  a. didn'ts
  b. did nots
  c. did not

5. don't
  a.
  b. do not

6. hadn't
  a. had not
  b. had nots
  c. hadn'ts

7. hasn't
  a. has nots
  b. has not
  c. hasnot

8. haven't
  a. have nots
  b. haven'ts
  c. have not

9. I'm
  a. I am
  b. I'ms
  c. I'am

10. I've
  a. I have
  b. I'ves
  c. I'have

11. isn't
  a. isn'ts
  b. is not
  c. is'not

12. let's
  a. lets
  b. let'us
  c. let us

13. mightn't
  a. mightnt
  b. might not
  c. might'not

14. mustn't
  a. mustnt
  b. must'not
  c. must not

Demonstrative Pronoun

This, That, These, and Those

Words that point to specific things are known as demonstrative pronouns. "This is a pencil," for example.

These pronouns indicate the relationship between the speaker and the object:

- this / these: an object or objects in close proximity to the person speaking (often within touching distance)
- that / those: an object or objects distant from the person speaking (often out of touching distance)
- that over there / those over there: object or objects located a long distance away from the person

1. _____ orange I'm eating is delicious.
    a. These
    b. This
    c. That

2. It is better than _____ apples from last week.
    a. that
    b. these
    c. those

3. Astronauts don't get fresh fruit like _____ peaches we are eating.
    a. this
    b. these
    c. that

4. _____ meals they take into space are freeze-dried.
    a. Those
    b. That
    c. This

5. _____ fact means they must add water to them.
    a. These
    b. This here
    c. That

6. _____ granola bars are tasty too.
    a. These
    b. Them
    c. This here

7. Don't sign me up for _____ next shuttle flight.
    a. these here
    b. that
    c. that there

8. _____ book is so heavy I can hardly lift it.
    a. Those
    b. This here
    c. This

9. Some believed _____ dream could be a reality.
    a. that there
    b. these
    c. that

10. _____ change is due to our astronauts.
    a. This
    b. That there
    c. These here

Refresher: Simple, Compound & Complex

A **clause** is a collection of related words that includes a subject and a verb. Clauses are classified into two types: **independent clauses** and **dependent clauses**. **Independent clauses** constitute a complete thought and can function independently. **Dependent clauses** contain a subject and a verb but do not function as a complete thought. Clauses are important to understand because they are the foundation of all sentence types. Now we'll look at the three different types of sentences.

Simple sentences are made up of a single independent clause. That's how easy they are! It has a subject and a verb. It completes the thought.

Compound sentences contain at least two independent clauses and no dependent clauses. To put it another way, a compound sentence is formed by combining at least two simple sentences.

Complex sentences have at least one independent clause and one dependent clause.

Clauses, which are written expressions that contain a subject and a verb, are the building blocks of all sentences. Dependent clauses cannot stand on their own, whereas independent clauses can. Sentences are classified into three types: simple, compound, and complex. Simple sentences are made up of a single independent clause. Compound sentences are also made up of two or more independent clauses. Complex sentences contain an independent clause as well as one or more dependent clauses.

1. **'Darkness cannot drive out darkness; only light can do that.' - Martin Luther King Jr.**
   a. Compound sentence
   b. Complex sentence
   c. Dependent clause

2. **'Beauty is in the heart of the beholder.' - H.G. Wells**
   a. Dependent clause
   b. Independent clause
   c. Simple sentence

3. **Their robot can follow a simple path through a maze.**
   a. compound sentence
   b. simple sentence
   c. complex sentence

4. **Kristina was late because she the traffic was terrible.**
   a. compound sentence
   b. complex sentence
   c. simple sentence

5. **He won the prize, but he was not happy.**
   a. complex sentence
   b. compound sentence
   c. simple sentence

6. **'Silence is golden when you can't think of a good answer.' - Muhammad Ali**
   a. Complex sentence
   b. Dependent clause
   c. Independent clause

7. **Although it was cold, we played the match.**
   a. Complex sentence
   b. Independent clause
   c. Dependent clause

8. **'People won't have time for you if you are always angry or complaining.' - Stephen Hawking**
   a. Simple sentence
   b. Independent clause
   c. Complex sentence

Tenses

Verbs are classified into three tenses: past, present, and future. The term "past" refers to events that have already occurred (e.g., earlier in the day, yesterday, last week, three years ago). The present tense is used to describe what is happening right now or what is ongoing. The future tense refers to events that have yet to occur (e.g., later, tomorrow, next week, next year, three years from now).

borrowed	went	eat	play	go	giving
read	give	gave	will eat	yelled	seeing
will have	had	reading	will go	do	will borrow
playing	doing	yelling	did	will yell	will do
will give	fight	borrow	yell	will fight	will play
borrowing	played	fighting	read	have	will see
going	see	will read	fought	eating	ate
saw	having				

Simple Present (11)	Present Progressive (IS/ARE +) (11)	Past (11)	Future (11)

Fictional vs. Fictitious vs. Fictive

Fictional is invented as part of a work of fiction

SYNONYMS:
Fabricated
Imaginary

Fictitious is created, taken, or assumed for the sake of concealment; not genuine; false

SYNONYMS:
Bogus
Counterfeit

Fictive - fictitious; imaginary. pertaining to the creation of fiction
- is capable of imaginative creation.

SYNONYMS:

Make-believe
Fabricated

1. He dismissed recent rumors about his private life as _____.
   a. fictitious
   b. fictional
   c. fictive

2. I have the impression that this _____ marriage of ours is like a ghost in a play.
   a. fictional
   b. fictitious
   c. fictive

3. The setting is a _____ island in the Chesapeake River.
   a. fictitious
   b. fictional
   c. fictive

4. The writer has _____ talent.
   a. fictitious
   b. fictional
   c. fictive

5. Almost all _____ detectives are unreal.
   a. fictitious
   b. fictional
   c. fictive

6. The names of the shops are entirely _____.
   a. fictive
   b. fictional
   c. fictitious

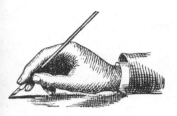

Fill-in The Appositive

Score: _____

Date: _____

Appositives are words or phrases that come before or after other nouns or pronouns to describe them further. The appositives should give the reader additional information about the nouns and pronouns in the sentences. Keep in mind that an appositive can be a single word or a group of words.

Appositives can be either essential or non-essential. If the appositive is required for the sentence to make sense, it is essential. This means it cannot be omitted. If the appositive is not required for the sentence's meaning and could be excluded, it is nonessential.

Commas should be used to separate non-essential appositives from the sentence. Commas are not used to separate essential appositives.

Examples:

Jane, my younger sister, is 27 years old. (Jane renames her younger sister)

My mother, who works as a nurse, has a red automobile. (A nurse renames mother, but this isn't necessary for the meaning of the line.)

Kevin is the name of the young artist that created this painting. (Who painted this image renames boy, which is crucial to the sentence's meaning.)

An insect, a ladybug, has just landed on the rose bush.

meadowlark	fiancé	cousin	valedictorian	Jones
champion	governor	movie	capital	

1. My uncle, the former _____ of Maine, loves ice cream

2. Sally's _____ Gerald works at Walmart

3. Providence, the _____ of RI, is a great city

4. We saw the state bird, the _____, at the park

5. My youngest _____ Caroline goes to Princeton University

6. Muhammad Ali, the three time heavy weight _____ of the world won a gold medal in 1960

7. Sally Smith, the _____, gave a wonderful speech at graduation

8. The vice principal, Mr. _____, suspended my brother

9. My favorite _____, "Stand and Deliver" always makes me cry.

Informational Text

An informational text is a nonfiction piece of writing that aims to educate or inform the reader about a specific topic. An informational text, unlike fiction or some other types of nonfiction texts, does not contain any characters. It presents information in a way that allows the reader to learn more about something of interest to them.

Informational text is a type of nonfiction that is intended to convey factual information about a specific topic. The purpose of informational text is to deliver information about a topic, and it is distinguished by its formatting, which includes organization, written cues (visual variations in text), and visuals/graphics.

Literary nonfiction, expository writing, persuasive/argumentative writing, and procedural writing are the four basic types of informational text. Examples of informational text can be found in a variety of formats both online and in print.

Select the best answer for each question.

1. **Identify the main idea: "You wouldn't use a nail file to peel carrots. You can't tune an engine with a cheese grater, either. So why would you buy a wrench to do the job of a screwdriver?"**
    a. Always use the right tool.
    b. Wrench and screwdrivers are basically the same.
    c. Use nail file for your fingernails.

2. **Autobiographies are written in which point of view?**
    a. second
    b. third
    c. first

3. **Differentiate between a plot and a theme.**
    a. A plot is the ending in a story, a theme conveys the message in first person
    b. A theme is a collection of the main idea, while a plot conveys the point of the ending
    c. A plot is more of what happens in a story, whereas a theme conveys the message of the story

4. **Which is not an article in a reference book?**
    a. thesaurus entry for the word army
    b. encyclopedia article on World War II
    c. a review of a novel

5. **When creating summaries, it's important to _____.**
    a. tell the ending of the story
    b. Write down the main points in your own words
    c. Use the first person exact words

6. **Which type of literary nonfiction is not meant to be published or shared?**
    a. biography
    b. diary
    c. memoir

7. **Which of the following should you do as you read an informational text?**
    a. Take notes
    b. find clue words and text
    c. read as quickly as possible

8. **What makes a speech different from an article?**
    a. speeches are meant to be spoken aloud to an audience
    b. speeches do not inform about a topic
    c. articles can persuade a reader

9. **Which type of literary nonfiction is a short piece on a single topic?**
    a. essay
    b. letter
    c. memoir

10. **Procedural writing example:**
    a. letter to the editor, blog entry
    b. textbook, travel brochure
    c. cookbooks, how-to articles, instruction manuals

Grammar Overview: Nouns, Verbs, Adjectives

A noun is a word that describes someone, a place, something, or an idea. Names, locations, physical objects, or objects and concepts that do not exist in the physical world, such as a dream or a theory, are examples of nouns. A noun is a single word, such as sister, home, desk, wedding, hope, pizza, or squirrel.

There are numerous ways to use nouns in language, and these various types of nouns are classified. In general, there are ten distinct types of nouns that are used in specific and unique contexts, but let's look at eight of them today.

Common Noun	a non-specific person, place, or thing	baby, mom
Compound Nouns	made up of two nouns	bus driver, sunflower
Collective Noun	group of individuals	team, family
Proper Noun	A specific person, place, or thing	Dr. Morgan, Amazon
Concrete Noun	identified through one of the five senses	air, chirps
Plural Noun	Multiple people, places, or things	bottles, pencils
Singular Noun	One person, place, or thing	chair, desk
Abstract Noun	things that don't exist as physical objects	fear, love

Common Noun: A generic name for a person, place, or thing in a class or group is a common noun. In contrast to proper nouns, common nouns are not capitalized unless they begin a sentence or appear in a title. All nouns fall into one of two categories: common or proper. Proper nouns are distinct from common nouns in that they name something specific. Nouns in common use do not. Unnecessary capitalization of common nouns is a common spelling error. Some words, such as president, seem to beg for a capital letter because we instinctively want to emphasize their significance. However, if it does not name something or someone specific, even this lofty title is a common noun (in this case, a specific president).

Compound Noun: Every compound noun is made up of two or more words that are combined to form a noun. These distinct words do not have to be nouns in and of themselves; all they need to do is communicate a specific person, place, idea, or thing. A compound noun can be a common noun (for example, fish sticks), a proper noun (for example, Pizza Hut), or an abstract noun (lovesickness). They can be hyphenated or not, and they can have a space between words—especially if one of the words has more than one syllable, as in living room. You'll start noticing compound nouns everywhere once you've learned to recognize them. Fire-flies? Compound noun. Sub sandwich? Compound noun. Software developer, mother-in-law, underworld, toothache, garlic knot? They are all compound nouns.

Collective Noun: A collective noun is a word or phrase that refers to a group of people or things as if they were a single entity. There are some exceptions to the rule that collective nouns are treated as singular. Collective nouns such as team, family, class, group, and host use a singular verb when the entity acts as a whole and a plural verb when the individuals who make up the entity act individually.

Collective nouns refer to more than one person or thing in a category. A pride cannot have just one lion, and a single flower does not make a bouquet. As a result, a collective noun always refers to a plurality of some kind.

Example: The group is working on a mural. (Because the mural is painted collectively by the group, the verb is singular.)

Example: The group cannot agree on how to paint the mural. (Because the group members disagree with one another, the verb is plural.)

Proper Noun: A proper noun is a name that is specific (as opposed to generic) to a specific person, place, or thing. In English, proper nouns are always capitalized, regardless of where they appear in a sentence. That is, whether it appears at the beginning, middle, or end of a sentence, it is always written with the first letter in capital letters. In a sentence, a proper noun is used to name a person, place, or organization, such as Jim, Molly, India, Germany, Amazon, Microsoft, and so on.

Concrete Noun: A concrete noun is one that can be identified using at least one of the five senses (taste, touch, sight, hearing, or smell). Objects and substances that we cannot perceive (see, hear, taste, touch, or smell) with our sense organs are NOT concrete nouns. The majority of nouns become concrete nouns because we can feel them (for example, all animals and people) with our sense organs. Concrete nouns can be common nouns, countable nouns, proper nouns, uncountable nouns, collective nouns, and so on. All nouns are classified into two types: concrete nouns and abstract nouns.

Abstract Nouns: An abstract noun is one that cannot be perceived through any of the five senses (i.e., taste, touch, sight, hearing, smelling). In other words, an abstract noun is a noun that exists only in our minds and cannot be recognized by our senses.

Concrete nouns are tangible, whereas <u>abstract nouns</u> are intangible.

Concrete nouns can be experienced with the five senses, whereas <u>abstract nouns</u> cannot.

Singular Noun: Singular nouns are used in sentences to refer to a single person, place, thing, or idea. Singular nouns include things like boy, girl, teacher, boat, goat, hand, and so on.

Plural noun: There are numerous plural noun rules, and because nouns are used so frequently in writing! The correct spelling of plurals is usually determined by what letter the singular noun ends in. Take a look at some examples.

Add s to the end of regular nouns to make them plural.

cat – cats

house – houses

If the singular noun ends in s, ss, sh, ch, x, or z, add es to make it plural.

bus – buses

lunch – lunches

Singular nouns ending in -s or -z may require you to double the -s or -z before adding the -es for pluralization in some cases.

quiz – quizzes

gas –gasses

If the noun ends in f or fe, the f is frequently changed to ve before adding the -s to form the plural form.

calf–calves

wife – wives

Exceptions:

roof – roofs

chef – chefs

When some nouns are pluralized, they do not change at all.

sheep – sheep

species – species

There are additional rules that we did not cover here. Please spend some time studying the following:

If the final letter of a singular noun is -y and the letter preceding the -y is a consonant, the noun ends in -y. puppy – puppies

If the singular noun ends in -y and the letter preceding the -y is a vowel, add an -s. boy – boys

If the singular noun ends in -o, make it plural by adding -es. potato – potatoes Exception: photo – photos

If a singular noun ends in -us, the plural ending is usually -i. cactus – cacti

When a singular noun ends in -is, the plural ending is -es. ellipsis – ellipses

If a singular noun ends in -on, the plural noun ends in -a. criterion – criteria

Verbs

In theory, verbs are easy to understand. A verb is a word that describes an action, an occurrence, or a state of being. Of course, there are many different types of verbs, but remember that a verb should indicate that something is happening because an action is taking place in some way. When first learning about verbs, many students simply refer to them as 'doing words,' because they always indicate that something has been done, is being done, or will be done in the future (depending on the tense that you are writing in).

Verbs, like nouns, are the main part of a sentence or phrase, telling a story about what is going on. In fact, full thoughts cannot be conveyed without a verb, and even the simplest sentences, such as (Kim sings.) Actually, a verb can be a sentence in and of itself, with the subject, in most cases you, implied, as in Sing! and Drive!

The location of the verb in relation to the subject is one clue that can help you identify it. Verbs are almost always followed by a noun or pronoun. The subject is made up of these nouns and pronouns.

1. Jim **eats** his dinner quickly.
2. We **went** to the bank.

Adjectives

Adjectives are descriptive words for nouns. A noun is defined as a person, place, thing, or idea. We want to be as descriptive as possible when we speak or write. Being descriptive allows the reader or listener to understand better what you are attempting to describe. You want your audience to have the best possible understanding of what you're describing.

Grammar Research

This worksheet is designed to encourage exploration, critical thinking, and a deeper appreciation of the history and diversity of grammar. Write your answers in your grammar notebook.

Research Task 1: The Evolution of English Grammar

- **Objective**: Research how English grammar has evolved from Old English to Modern English.

- **Instructions**:

   1. Look up information about the grammar of Old English (around 5th to 11th century).

   2. Compare it with the grammar rules of Modern English.

   3. Write a short paragraph highlighting three major changes in grammar rules over time.

Research Task 2: Grammar in Different Cultures

- **Objective**: Understand how grammar rules can vary in different languages.

- **Instructions**:

   1. Select two languages other than English.

   2. Research the basic grammar structure of these languages (e.g., sentence structure, verb conjugation).

   3. Write a comparison of these grammar structures with English grammar.

Research Task 3: The Role of Technology in Grammar

- **Objective**: Explore how technology has influenced grammar learning and usage in recent times.

- **Instructions**:

   1. Investigate the impact of digital communication (like texting and social media) on grammar.

   2. Look into one or two grammar-checking tools (like Grammarly or Microsoft Editor).

   3. Discuss how these technological advances have changed the way we use and learn grammar.

Reflection Questions

1. What was the most surprising thing you learned about the history of grammar?

2. How do you think grammar will continue to evolve with technology?

3. Which grammar rule from another language did you find most interesting and why?

NO ANSWER KEY

Homophones - Words that are pronounced the same but they have different meanings.

Name: _____

Date: _____

Match the homophones.

1	☐	oar	there	A
2	☐	pair	prey	B
3	☐	plain	soul	C
4	☐	pray	stationery	D
5	☐	profit	week	E
6	☐	right	write	F
7	☐	sail	sun	G
8	☐	seam	sight	H
9	☐	sow	sale	I
10	☐	sole	seem	J
11	☐	son	or	K
12	☐	stationary	prophet	L
13	☐	suite	weight	M
14	☐	their	toe	N
15	☐	two	sweet	O
16	☐	wait	pear	P
17	☐	weak	plane	Q

Identify The Various Parts of Grammar

Across

1. the first word in a noun group
2. a word used to describe a noun
3. the first part of a sentence is called the ....
7. this tells us how many of a noun (some / ten / a few)
10. a sentence that uses a conjunction to join two independent clauses
11. a sentence with a dependent clause and one or more independent clauses
12. one conjunction is ....
15. a clause beginning with if / when / because is called ....
18. the last part of a sentence is called ....
19. a phrase beginning with a preposition is called ....

Down

3. What type of sentence is one independent clause
4. an independent clause can only have one ....
5. The last word of a noun group
6. a / an / the are called
8. this / that / these / those are called ....
9. tells us who owns the noun
13. we change the verb to make past ....
14. a story written or spoken in past tense
16. a clause that contains the full meaning is called ....
20. the conjunctions so and because give us a result and ....

ADJECTIVE INDEPENDENT
COMPLEX TENSE DEPENDENT
BECAUSE VERB
POSSESSIVE QUANTIFIER
COMPOUND SIMPLE
PREPOSITIONAL RECOUNT
DETERMINER ARTICLE
OBJECT REASON SUBJECT
DEMONSTRATIVE NOUN

Mood and Modality in Verbs

Score: _____

Date: _____

Mood in verbs refers to the form a verb takes to express the attitude of the speaker towards the action or state the verb describes. Modality, on the other hand, refers to the manner in which the action or state is experienced or intended. In English, there are primarily three moods: indicative, imperative, and subjunctive.

1. **Indicative Mood:**

   - **Description:** The indicative mood is used for statements of fact or belief, questions, and generally for most statements in everyday speech or writing.

      - **Example:** "The cat sleeps on the mat."

2. **Imperative Mood:**

   - **Description:** The imperative mood is used for commands, instructions, requests, or suggestions.

      - **Example:** "Please close the door."

3. **Subjunctive Mood:**

   - **Description:** The subjunctive mood is used to express wishes, hypotheticals, conditions contrary to fact, and necessity. It's often seen in clauses beginning with "if" or "that."

      - **Example:** "If I were a bird, I could fly."

Multiple Choice Questions

1. In the sentence "I suggest that he speak with the manager," which mood is the verb "speak" in?

(a) Indicative (b) Imperative (c) Subjunctive   (d) None of the above

2. Which mood is used in the sentence "Do your homework before going out"?

(a) Indicative (b) Imperative (c) Subjunctive   (d) None of the above

True or False

1. The sentence "It is essential that she be informed immediately" uses the indicative mood. **T or F**

2. "He runs five miles every day" is an example of the imperative mood. **T or F**

Short Answer Questions

1. Write a sentence using the subjunctive mood.

----

2. How does the imperative mood change the tone of a sentence?

Nouns, Adverbs, and Verbs Review

SCORE_____

DATE_____

Nouns

Nouns are words that name people, places, things, or ideas. There are several types of nouns, including common nouns (general names like 'dog', 'city'), proper nouns (specific names like 'Fido', 'New York'), and abstract nouns (names for ideas or qualities like 'happiness', 'strength').

Adverbs

Adverbs modify verbs, adjectives, or other adverbs. They often tell how, when, where, why, or to what extent something happens. For example, in the sentence "She sings beautifully," 'beautifully' is an adverb describing how she sings.

Verbs

Verbs are action words. They describe what someone or something is doing. Verbs can show actions (run, jump), states of being (is, seem), or help other verbs (has, do).

Nouns Questions

1. Identify the noun in this sentence: "The cat slept on the mat." _____

2. Is 'happiness' a common noun, a proper noun, or an abstract noun? _____

3. Choose the noun from this list: quickly, large, car, blue. _____

4. Which of the following is a proper noun: river, Amazon River, water? _____

5. Create a sentence using 'freedom' as a noun.

6. In the sentence "She gave her friend a gift," which word is a noun? _____

7. Identify all the nouns in the sentence: "The teacher read a book to the class." _____

8. Challenge: Is 'music' a tangible or an abstract noun?_____

9. Write a sentence where 'light' is used as a noun. _____

10. Choose the noun from these options: beautifully, elephant, quickly, softly. _____

Adverbs Questions

1. Identify the adverb in this sentence: "He ran quickly to the store." _____

2. Create a sentence using 'silently' as an adverb. _____

3. Which word is the adverb in this sentence: "She spoke softly to the baby"? _____

4. Choose the adverb from this list: happy, happiness, happily, happinesses. _____

5. In the sentence "The dog barked loudly," what does the adverb describe? _____

6. Challenge: Is 'extremely' an adverb of manner, place, or degree? _____

7. Write a sentence where 'yesterday' is used as an adverb. _____

8. Identify the adverb in the sentence: "The flowers here grow abundantly." _____

9. Which word is an adverb in the following sentence: "The movie was incredibly exciting." _____

10. Create a sentence using 'often' as an adverb.

_____

Verbs Questions

1. Identify the verb in this sentence: "The bird flies high." _____

2. Create a sentence using 'dance' as a verb. _____

3. In the sentence "She can sing beautifully," which word is the verb? _____

4. Choose the verb from this list: quickly, sing, happy, under. _____

5. Write a sentence where 'think' is used as a verb. _____

6. In the sentence "The sun rises in the east," what is the verb? _____

7. Identify all the verbs in this sentence: "He walked to the store and bought milk."

_____

8. Challenge: Is 'was' an action verb or a state of being verb? _____

9. Create a sentence using 'study' as a verb.

_____

10. In the sentence "They have finished their work," which word is the main verb? _____

Parallel Structure in Writing

Imagine being on a seesaw. For it to work perfectly, both sides need to be balanced, right? That's exactly what parallel structure is in writing - balance!

Parallel structure means using the same pattern of words to show that two or more ideas have the same level of importance. This can happen at the word, phrase, or clause level.

Let's pretend we're making a sandwich. Just like how you would put the same ingredients (like a slice of cheese or a piece of lettuce) on both halves of the bread, in parallel structure, you use the same type of words (like verbs or nouns) in the same order.

For example, without parallel structure, a sentence might be: "I like running, to bake, and how I can paint." This sentence is a bit like a sandwich with cheese, a whole tomato, and sliced ham. It doesn't quite fit together, does it?

But with parallel structure, the sentence becomes: "I like running, baking, and painting." Now, it's a well-made sandwich! All the verbs are in the '-ing' form, just like how all the ingredients in your sandwich might be sliced.

Here's another example:

Not Parallel: "She enjoys reading, baking, and to play guitar." Parallel: "She enjoys reading, baking, and playing guitar."

Activity:

1. Try writing a sentence about your favorite hobbies using parallel structure.

   ----

2. Correct the following sentence: "He likes playing football, swimming, and to ride a bicycle."

Remember, the parallel structure makes your sentences clear and balanced, just like a perfect seesaw or a well-made sandwich!

Possessive nouns, Pronouns, Plural Nouns Review

SCORE_____

DATE_____

Possessive Nouns

Possessive nouns show ownership or belonging. They are usually formed by adding an apostrophe and an "s" ('s) to a singular noun, or just an apostrophe (') to a plural noun that already ends in "s".

Singular Possessive Noun: Add 's
- Example: The dog's leash (the leash belongs to the dog).

Plural Possessive Noun: Add only an apostrophe if the noun ends in "s".
- Example: The dogs' leashes (the leashes belong to multiple dogs).

Pronouns

Pronouns are words that replace nouns in a sentence. They can refer to specific people or things.

Subject Pronouns: Used as the subject of a sentence (I, you, he, she, it, we, they).
- Example: She is reading a book.

Object Pronouns: Used as the object of a verb or preposition (me, you, him, her, it, us, them).
- Example: The teacher called him.

Plural Nouns

Plural nouns refer to more than one person, place, thing, or idea. Most nouns become plural by adding "s" or "es".

Regular Plural Nouns: Add "s" or "es".
- Example: Cat → Cats, Box → Boxes.

Irregular Plural Nouns: Change the word form.
- Example: Child → Children, Mouse → Mice.

Possessive Nouns

1. Fill in the blank with the correct possessive form: "This is the _____ (bicycle) helmet."

2. Choose the correct possessive noun: "The _____ tail was wagging happily." (dog/dog's/dogs')

3. Rewrite the sentence using a possessive noun: "The hat of the man was left on the table."

_____

4. Identify the possessive noun in the sentence: "Sarah's book is on the desk."_____

5. Correct the error in the sentence: "The childrens' playground is newly renovated."_____

Pronouns

1. Replace the underlined word(s) with the correct pronoun: "John and Mary said that <u>John and Mary</u> would come to the party." _____

2. Choose the correct pronoun to complete the sentence: "Neither of the cakes is mine; _____ is the pie." (it/they/she)

3. Fill in the blank with an appropriate pronoun: "Everyone forgot his or her homework, but I remembered _____."

4. Identify the type of pronoun (subject, object, possessive) in the sentence: "Ours is the last house on the left."

5. Rewrite the sentence using a pronoun: "The children played in the park, and the children had a lot of fun."

_____

Plural Nouns

1. Write the plural form of "fox." _____

2. Identify the plural noun in the sentence: "There are several books on the shelf." _____

3. Correct the plural noun in the sentence: "The childs played in the yard." _____

4. Choose the correct plural form: "The _____ are migrating south." (goose/geese)

5. Rewrite the sentence making the underlined word plural: "The woman is walking her <u>dog</u>."

_____

Reading Comprehension
Alphabetical Order

1. Which word follows "engage" in the dictionary?
   a. encounter
   b. erase
   c. energy
   d. emigrant

2. Which word would follow "honor" in the dictionary?
   a. hiccup
   b. hesitate
   c. humble
   d. hideout

3. Which word would follow "linoleum" in the dictionary?
   a. literature
   b. lightning
   c. lilac
   d. liberty

4. Which word would follow "minute" in the dictionary?
   a. method
   b. mimic
   c. misery
   d. minister

5. Which word would follow "pleasure" in the dicitonary?
   a. pliers
   b. photo
   c. platinum
   d. place

6. What word follows "proceed" in the dictionary?
   a. product
   b. program
   c. probable
   d. priority

7. What word follow "respiration" in the dictionary?
   a. resound
   b. resign
   c. resort
   d. respond

8. What word follows "sneeze" in the dictionary?
   a. slumber
   b. snarl
   c. snatch
   d. snorkel

9. What word follows "territory" in the dictionary?
   a. textile
   b. terrific
   c. telescope
   d. tarnish

10. What word follows "curtain" in the dictionary?
   a. crumble
   b. curse
   c. cube
   d. customer

Root Words, Prefixes, and Suffixes

- A **root word** is the basic form of a word that can stand alone or form the basis of new words through the addition of prefixes and suffixes.

- A **prefix** is a group of letters added to the beginning of a word to change its meaning.

- A **suffix** is a group of letters added to the end of a word to change its meaning or grammatical function.

Examples:

- Root word: "write"

  With Prefix: "prewrite" (before writing)

  With Suffix: "writer" (someone who writes)

- Root word: "happy"

  With Prefix: "unhappy" (not happy)

  With Suffix: "happiness" (the state of being happy)

Check Your Knowledge Questions:

1. What does the prefix "un-" mean in the word "unbelievable"?

A) Not   B) Before C) Many D) Without

2. The word "careless" means "full of care." <u>True</u> / <u>False</u>

3. Add a suffix to "hope" to make a noun meaning "the state of having hope." "Hope_____"

4. Short Answer: Identify the root word in "disagreement." Explain how the prefix and suffix change its meaning.

5. Match the prefix/suffix to its meaning:

A) "pre-"	1. Again
B) "-able"	2. Before
C) "re-"	3. Capable of
D) "-ness"	4. State of

Sentence Fragments and Run-on Sentences

READ ONLY ACTIVITY

SCORE_____

DATE_____

In the bustling city of Grammaropolis, two notorious characters often confuse the residents: **Sentence Fragment** and **Run-on Sentence**.

Sentence Fragment, a mischievous little one, was known for leaving things half-done. He was like a puzzle with missing pieces. His sentences were incomplete, lacking either a subject (who or what the sentence is about) or a predicate (what the subject is doing or being).

For instance, Sentence Fragment would say, "Went to the park." Here, we're left wondering who went to the park? A subject is missing!

Run-on Sentence, the over-enthusiastic talker, was infamous for his endless chatter. He was like a train with too many carriages connected without proper couplings. His sentences had too many ideas all jumbled together without the correct punctuation or conjunctions.

For example, Run-on Sentence would say, "I love ice cream it's so delicious my favorite flavor is chocolate." Here, there are separate ideas that need to be properly connected or divided. A better way of writing this is... I love ice cream; it's so delicious, and my favorite flavor is chocolate.

Mind Exercise:

1. Identify if the following sentences are Sentence Fragments or Run-on Sentences:

    a. "Because it was sunny outside."

    b. "I enjoy reading books I also play football."

2. How would you rewrite the sentences above to make them complete and well-structured?

Answers:

1. a. Sentence Fragment - It lacks a main clause. Who did what because it was sunny outside?

    b. Run-on Sentence - There are two separate ideas that need to be properly connected or divided.

2. a. Because it was sunny outside, we decided to have a picnic.

    b. I enjoy reading books, and I also play football.

A **sentence fragment** is incomplete and is missing either a subject, verb, or a complete thought. To correct a sentence fragment, you need to identify what's missing and add it. **Example**: *In the park*. **Correction**: *The children are playing in the park*.

A **run-on sentence** contains multiple independent clauses (complete sentences) that are not properly connected or separated. To correct this, you can - **1.** Split the run-on sentence into separate sentences using periods. **2.** Use a comma followed by a coordinating conjunction (for, and, nor, but, or, yet, so) to connect the clauses. **3.** Use a semicolon to separate the independent clauses if they are closely related and balanced. **Example**: Run-on: *I love reading books I also play football*. **Corrections**: **1.** *I love reading books. I also play football*. **2.** *I love reading books, and I also play football*. **3.** *I love reading books; I also play football*.

Subject-Verb Agreement

Welcome, boys and girls, to the Great Grammar Circus! Today, we will see the amazing acrobats of grammar: Subjects and Verbs. They need to work together perfectly to keep the grammar circus running smoothly. This teamwork is called Subject-Verb Agreement!

Act 1: Meet the Performers – Subjects and Verbs

First, let's meet our stars. The Subject is who or what the sentence is about, like *the clown*, *the elephants*, or *Lily*. The Verb is the action or state of being, like *juggles*, *trumpets*, or *is*.

When they perform together, they must agree on a number. If the subject is singular (one), the verb must be singular. If the subject is plural (more than one), the verb must be plural."

Act 2: The Singular Spectacle

In the spotlight is the singular performer. When we have one subject, like *the juggler*, our verb is also singular, like *juggles*.

For example:

- The juggler **juggles**.

- A dog **barks**.

Activity: Singular Star Creation. Create 3 sentences with singular subjects and verbs, then illustrate them for extra credit!

Act 3: The Plural Parade

Now, behold the plural parade! When we have more than one subject, like *the acrobats*, our verb is also plural, like *perform*.

For example:

- The acrobats **perform** amazing feats.

- Dogs **bark** at night.

Activity: Plural Party. Write 3 sentences with plural subjects and verbs. For extra credit, use colorful pens or stickers to decorate!

Finale: The Subject-Verb Agreement Showdown

Now, for the grand finale, let's see if our subjects and verbs can stay in perfect harmony. Remember, they must match in number to keep the Grammar Circus balance.

Activity: The Great Grammar Showdown. Write a sentence and ask a friend or family member to check if your subject and verb agree. If they do, give yourself a round of applause!

And that's a wrap for today at the Great Grammar Circus! Remember, like the best circus performers, subjects and verbs must always work together in agreement. Keep practicing, and soon, you'll be a grammar acrobat too!

Final Extra Credit Challenge: Create your own mini circus story using correct subject-verb agreement. Share your story with the class, and let the grammar fun continue!

Use this section below to complete your Fun Activity & Extra Credit work

Test Your Knowledge

SCORE_____

DATE_____

Part 1: Parts of Speech

1. A noun is a word that describes an action or a state of being.

True	False

2. Which of the following is an adjective?

A. Run	B. Quickly	C. Blue

3. Identify the verb in this sentence: "The cat slept on the warm, sunny windowsill."

Part 2: Verb Tenses

4. The past perfect tense describes an action that will happen in the future.

True	False

5. What is the present progressive tense of the verb "to run"?

6. Fill in the blank with the correct form of the verb "to go": "By the time we arrived at the cinema, the movie _____ already started."

Part 3: Sentence Structure

7. A compound sentence contains two or more independent clauses and one or more dependent clauses.

True	False

8. Identify the subject in this sentence: "In the garden, the beautiful flowers bloom brightly."

9. Write a complex sentence using the word "although."

Part 4: Punctuation

10. A semicolon can be used to connect two closely related independent clauses.

True	False

11. Which of the following sentences is punctuated correctly? A. "Let's eat grandma!" B. "Let's eat, grandma!"

12. Correct the punctuation in this sentence: "She said I'm sorry for your loss."

This, That, These, and Those

This, that, these and those are demonstratives. We use this, that, these, and those to point to people and things. This and that are singular. These and those are plural.

1. _____ orange I'm eating is delicious.
   a. This
   b. These
   c. Those
   d. That

2. It is better than _____ apples from last week.
   a. that
   b. those
   c. these
   d. this

3. Let's exchange _____ bread for these crackers.
   a. those
   b. this
   c. these
   d. that

4. Let's try some of _____ freeze-dried steak.
   a. this
   b. this here
   c. them
   d. those there

5. Is _____ water boiling yet?
   a. these here
   b. that
   c. that there
   d. this here

6. _____ granola bars are tasty too.
   a. These
   b. This here
   c. Them
   d. These here

7. _____ mountains don't look that far away.
   a. This
   b. Those
   c. These
   d. That

8. I like _____ pictures better than those.
   a. this
   b. that
   c. those
   d. these

9. _____ car at the far end of the lot is mine.
   a. That
   b. This
   c. These
   d. Those

10. I like the feel of _____ fabric.
   a. those
   b. this here
   c. that there
   d. this

11. In _____ early days, space travel was a dream.
   a. that
   b. them
   c. those
   d. this

12. _____ days, we believe humans will go to Mars.
   a. These
   b. This
   c. Those
   d. That

Understanding Conjunctions

SCORE_____

DATE_____

Conjunctions are words used to connect clauses, sentences, or words. They are essential in forming complex sentences and adding coherence to writing. There are three main types of conjunctions: coordinating, subordinating, and correlative.

1. **Coordinating Conjunctions:** These conjunctions connect elements of equal importance. The acronym FANBOYS (For, And, Nor, But, Or, Yet, So) helps remember them.

2. **Subordinating Conjunctions:** These are used to join an independent clause and a dependent clause. Examples include because, although, since, unless.

3. **Correlative Conjunctions:** These come in pairs and link equivalent elements. Examples are either...or, neither...nor, not only...but also.

Examples:

- **Coordinating**: "She was late, but she still caught the bus."

- **Subordinating**: "Although he was tired, he finished his homework."

- **Correlative**: "Neither the rain nor the wind stopped them."

Multiple Choice Questions:

1. Which of the following is a coordinating conjunction?

   A) Because

   B) And

   C) Although

   D) Unless

2. Identify the type of conjunction in this sentence: "She will succeed because she works hard."

   A) Coordinating

   B) Subordinating

   C) Correlative

   D) None of the above

3. Choose the correct correlative conjunction pair to complete the sentence: "_____ did he call me, _____ he sent a text."

   A) Either...or

   B) Not only...but also

   C) Both...and

   D) Neither...nor

True or False:

1. "Yet" can be used as a coordinating conjunction. TRUE or FALSE

2. A subordinating conjunction can appear at the start of a sentence. TRUE or FALSE

3. "Whether...or" is an example of a coordinating conjunction. TRUE or FALSE

Short Answer Questions:

1. Create a sentence using "but" as a coordinating conjunction.

----

2. Explain the difference between coordinating and subordinating conjunctions.

----

3. Use "neither...nor" in a sentence.

Extra Credit Conjunctions Writing Exercise

Objective: To practice using coordinating, subordinating, and correlative conjunctions in sentences and short paragraphs.

Instructions: Exercise should be done on separate sheet of paper.

1. **Coordinating Conjunctions:** Write five sentences using a different coordinating conjunction in each sentence. Remember the acronym FANBOYS (For, And, Nor, But, Or, Yet, So) to help you.

Example: "I wanted to play outside, but it was raining."

2. **Subordinating Conjunctions:** Write a short paragraph (4-5 sentences) on any topic of your choice. Include at least three different subordinating conjunctions (such as because, although, since, unless, etc.) in your paragraph.

Example topic: "A day at the beach"

Example sentence: "Although it was sunny, the water was surprisingly cold."

Verb Tenses (Past, Present, Future)

"Hello, young explorers! Today, we're going to be time travelers, exploring the past, present, and future. But how, you ask? With the help of our magical verbs! Verbs are not just action words; they are time machines that can take us anywhere in time!"

Part 1: Present Tense - The Here and Now

We start our adventure right here, right now, in the Present Tense. When we use present tense verbs, we talk about things happening currently, at this very moment. It's like looking at a snapshot of what's happening.

For example:

'I **eat** a sandwich.' (Happening now)

'The dog **barks** loudly.' (Happening now)

Fun Activity: Let's play 'Present Tense Charades'. Act out an action and let your friends or family guess the verb in the present tense!

Part 2: Past Tense - Our Yesterday's Tale

Next, we hop into our time machine and zoom back to the Past Tense. This is where we talk about things that have already happened, our past adventures.

For example:

'I **ate** a sandwich.' (Happened already)

'The dog **barked** loudly.' (Happened already)

Fun Activity: Create a 'Past Tense Diary'. Draw or write about something fun you did yesterday using past tense verbs!

Part 3: Future Tense - A Peek into Tomorrow

And now, let's fast-forward into the future with Future Tense. Here, we talk about actions that haven't happened yet but will happen.

For example:

'I **will eat** a sandwich.' (Will happen later)

'The dog **will bark** loudly.' (Will happen later)

Fun Activity: Future Tense Time Capsule. Write a letter to your future self using future tense verbs. What do you think you will be doing next year?"

Congratulations, time travelers! You've just explored the different times of verbs. Remember:

- Present Tense is like a snapshot of now.

- Past Tense is like a memory from yesterday.

- Future Tense is like a dream about tomorrow.

Extra Credit Challenge: Write three sentences about your day – one in the present tense, one in the past tense, and one in the future tense.

Learning about verb tenses is like having a time machine at your fingertips. Every time you use a verb, think about which time you're traveling to. Happy time traveling with verbs!

Use this section below to complete your Fun Activity & Extra Credit work

Alphabetize and Define

| meter |
| irony |
| personification |
| denotation |
| onomatopoeia |
| alliteration |
| rhyme |
| metaphor |
| theme |
| symbolism |
| repetition |
| simile |
| stanza |
| connotation |
| imagery |

1. _____

2. _____

3. _____

4. _____

5. _____

6. _____

7. _____

8. _____

9. _____

10. _____

11. _____

12. _____

13. _____

14. _____

15. _____

After putting the words in alphabetical order, choose 5 and write a definition in the space provided.

_____

_____

_____

_____

Apostrophe

An apostrophe is a punctuation mark used to indicate where something has been removed. It can be used in contractions, to show possession, to replace a phrase, for the plural form of family names, for irregular plural possessives, and, on rare occasions, to provide clarity for a non-possessive plural. Avoid common apostrophe mistakes, such as using 'it's' for the possessive 'its,' which should be 'its.' Omitting the apostrophe, putting it in the wrong place for a possessive plural, and using 'of' when you mean to contract a word with 'have' are other common errors.

Apostrophes, like any other aspect of language, are prone to errors. The omission of the apostrophe is one of the most common.

Here are some examples:

'Let's go to McDonalds.' **Correct**: 'McDonald's'
'Whos responsible for the bill?' **Correct**: 'Who's'
'Its about five o'clock.' **Correct**: 'It's.' We are saying 'it is' here, so we need the apostrophe.

1. **Where should the apostrophe go in didnt?**
   a. didn't
   b. did'nt

2. **How do you make the contraction for was not?**
   a. was'nt
   b. wasn't

3. **How do you make Jimmy possessive?**
   a. Jimmy's
   b. Jimmys

4. **Where should the apostrophe go in shouldnt?**
   a. should'nt
   b. shouldn't

5. **How do you make the contraction for she would?**
   a. she'd
   b. sh'ed

6. **What is the correct use of the apostrophe?**
   a. brother's toys
   b. brother'is toys

7. **Which of the following is the correct way to show possession with a plural noun ending in 's'?**
   a. Add an apostrophe at the end.
   b. No apostrophe is required.

8. **How would you express the plural possessive of the word 'child'?**
   a. Child's
   b. Children's

9. **What is the proper way to contract the possessive form of 'it'?**
   a. Its
   b. It's

10. **The _____ awfully good today.**
    a. weather
    b. weather's

11. **Adam believes _____ going to snow later.**
    a. it's
    b. its

12. **The dog was wagging _____ tail excitedly.**
    a. its
    b. it's

13. **Where did you leave _____ book?**
    a. your
    b. you're

14. **_____ going to Ms. Katy's room.**
    a. Wer'e
    b. We're

15. **Bobby always kicks _____ dolls around.**
    a. Kim and Sandy's
    b. Jennifer and Katie

16. **_____ not allowed to listen to music while they read.**
    a. They're
    b. Their're

Grammar Review

Common & Proper Noun: A noun is a word that is used to describe a person, animal, place, thing, or idea. **Common nouns** are words that are used to refer to general objects rather than specific ones. All of these items are named with common nouns: lamp, chair, couch, TV, window, painting, pillow, and candle.

A **proper noun** is a unique (not generic) name for a specific person, place, or thing. In English, proper nouns are always capitalized, regardless of where they appear in a sentence.

Common noun: I want to be a **writer**. ✓
Proper noun: Carlyon Jones wrote many books. ✓

Plural Nouns: Plural nouns are words that indicate the presence of more than one person, animal, place, thing, or idea.

- bottle – bottles. ✓
- cup – cups. ✓

Collective Nouns: Collective nouns are names for a collection or a number of people or things.

 crowd, government, team, family, audience, etc.

Singular Possessive Noun: A **singular possessive noun** indicates that something is owned by someone or something. We add an's to indicate ownership. • *cat's tail*, for example.

Concrete Noun: A **concrete noun** is a real-world physical object, such as a dog, a ball, or an ice cream cone. Another way to put it, a concrete noun is the name of an object which may be perceived by one or more of the five senses. An **abstract noun** is a concept or idea that does not exist in the physical world and cannot be touched, such as freedom, sadness, or permission.

Verb: A verb is defined as a word (such as jump, think, happen, or exist) that expresses an action and is usually one of the main parts of a sentence.

Adjectives are words that describe the qualities or states of being of nouns: enormous, doglike, silly, yellow, fun, fast.

Simple Subject: A **simple subject** is a subject's main word or words. It lacks any modifiers that could be used to describe the subject. To find the simple subject in a sentence, consider who or what is doing the action in the sentence. But keep in mind that a simple subject is very basic, a subject, a verb, and a completed thought.

Tina waited for the train.
"Tina" = subject, "waited" = verb ✓

Prepositions Object: A preposition is a word that appears before a noun to indicate its relationship to another word in the phrase or clause.
As a result, a noun can serve as the object of the preposition. The noun that follows the preposition is known as the object of the preposition.

To find the preposition's object:

1) Locate the preposition.
2) Then, put the preposition in the blank and ask "_____ who or what?"

Jim's house is across the street. (Across what?) street ✓
The show will begin at 7:00. (At what?) 7:00 ✓

Indirect Object: An indirect object is one that is used with a transitive verb to indicate who benefits from or receives something as a result of an action. In the sentence 'She gave him her address,' for example, 'him' is the indirect object.

Direct object: A direct object is a word or phrase that receives the verb's action. The direct object in the sentence: 'The kids eat cake.' is cake; the verb is eat, and the object being eaten is cake.

Direct Address: Nouns of **direct address** are the nouns used to indicate that a speaker is directly addressing a person or group. When addressing a person or thing directly, the name must be separated by a comma (or commas if in the middle of a sentence).

- Tommy, are you leaving so soon? ✓ (As "Tommy" is being addressed directly, his name is offset with a comma.)

1. **His father is the coach of the team.**
   a. his, father, team
   b. his, father, coach
   c. father, coach, team

2. **David is driving to the beach.**
   a. David, driving, beach
   b. David, driving
   c. David, beach

3. **What are the PROPER nouns in the following sentence?   My grandparents live in Florida.**
   a. grandparents, Flordia
   b. Flordia
   c. My, grandparents

4. **What are all the COMMON nouns in the following sentence?   I have two dogs and one cat.**
   a. cat, one
   b. dogs, cat
   c. I, dogs

5. **Which sentence contains only one common noun and one proper noun?**
   a. These potatoes are from Idaho.
   b. Casey is a talented singer and dancer.
   c. I live near the border of Nevada and Utah.

6. **Which sentence contains the correct form of a plural noun?**
   a. The wolves chase a frightened rabbit.
   b. The wolfes chase a frightened rabbit.
   c. The wolfs chase a frightened rabbit.

7. **Which sentence contains one singular noun and one plural noun?**
   a. The musician tunes her instrument.
   b. The conductor welcomes each musician.
   c. The singers walk across the stage.

8. **Identify the collective noun in the following sentence.**
   Derek is the lead singer in a band.
   a. singer
   b. band
   c. lead

9. **Which sentence contains the correct form of a singular possessive noun?**

    a. The boxs' lid is torn.

    b. The box's lid is torn.

    c. The boxes' lid is torn.

10. **Which sentence contains one concrete noun and on abstract noun?**

    a. John feels anxiety about meeting new people.

    b. The young boy plays with trains.

    c. The sand feels warm between my toes.

11. **Identify the simple subject in the following sentence.   The children are playing tag.**

    a. tag

    b. children

    c. The children

12. **Identify the simple subject in the following sentence.
    This computer belongs to my father.**

    a. computer

    b. This computer

    c. father

13. **Which sentence has an object of a preposition?**

    a. Several passengers missed the flight.

    b. Seattle is a city in Washington.

    c. The boys are racing remote-controlled cars.

14. **Identify the object of preposition in the following sentence.
    The are playing a game of cards.**

    a. cards

    b. game

    c. of cards

15. **Identify the subject complement in the following sentence.
    Mr. Smith is a talented poet.**

    a. poet

    b. talented

    c. Mr. Smith

16. **Identify the subject complement in the following sentence.
    Tulips and daisies are my favorite flowers.**

    a. my

    b. flowers

    c. favorite

17. **Identify the direct object in the following sentence.   Tyler delivers newspapers each morning.**

    a. newspapers

    b. morning

    c. each

18. **Identify the direct object in the following sentence.   We will paint the bathroom beige.**

    a. bathroom

    b. paint

    c. beige

19. **Identify the indirect object in the following sentence.   Mr. Jackson gave the students their grades.**

    a. grades

    b. students

    c. their

20. **Identify the indirect object in the following sentence.   Mrs. Parker bought her husband a new tie.**

    a. new tie

    b. husband

    c. tie

21. **In which sentence is paint used as a noun?**

    a. These artists paint the most amazing murals.

    b. We need two cans of brown paint.

    c. Let's paint the bedroom light green.

22. **In which sentence is sign used as a verb?**

    a. I saw it as a sign of good luck.

    b. Joelle is learning sign language.

    c. Did you sign the letter at the bottom?

23. **In which sentence is file used as an adjective?**

    a. This file contains the detective's notes.

    b. Put these papers in a file folder.

    c. I use a file to smooth the edges of my nails.

24. **Identify the direct address in the following sentence.** This is your baseball bat, Kenny.

    a. Kenny

    b. baseball

    c. bat

25. **Identify the direct address in the following sentence.**
    Hector, did you buy more milk?

    a. Hector

    b. you

    c. milk

26. **Objects of the preposition. Lee cried during the movie.**

    a. Lee

    b. movie

    c. cried

27. **Objects of the preposition. The phone is on the table.**

    a. table

    b. phone

    c. none

28. **Direct Objects: Every actor played his part.**

    a. his part

    b. actor

    c. played

29. **Direct Objects: The crowd will cheer the President.**

    a. the President

    b. cheer

    c. crowd

30. **Examples of concrete nouns are:**

    a. flower, music, bear, pie,

    b. love, cars, them, went

    c. me, I, she, they

31. **Direct Address: Well certainly, Mother, I remember what you said.**

    a. you

    b. Mother

    c. certainly

32. **Direct Address: I heard exactly what you said, Pam.**

    a. Pam

    b. none

    c. you

33. **Collective Noun: A choir of singers**

    a. choir

    b. sing

    c. singers

34. **Collective Noun: A litter of puppies**

    a. litter

    b. puppies

    c. puppy

Exploring the Nuances of Advanced Parts of Speech Answer Key:

Multiple Choice Questions

c) Who

Explanation: 'Who' is used to refer to people in relative clauses.

c) Might

Explanation: 'Might' is a modal verb expressing possibility.

True or False

True

Explanation: 'Regularly' is used to describe how often something happens.

False

Explanation: Phrasal verbs can consist of a verb and an adverb, a verb and a preposition, or a verb with both.

Short Answer Questions

Example Answer: "The task was extremely difficult; nevertheless, she completed it on time."
- Explanation: 'Nevertheless' is used here as an adverb to indicate contrast in degree.

Student's Own Answer (Note: This is a trick question. 'Underneath' is not a demonstrative pronoun.)
- • Expected Response: Correction that 'underneath' is not a demonstrative pronoun, but rather a preposition or adverb.

Prepositions of Place and Direction Answer Key:

Multiple Choice Questions

c) In
- Explanation: 'In' is used to indicate that something is within the confines of an area or a space.

a) into
- Explanation: 'Into' indicates movement from the outside to the inside of a place.

True or False

True
- Explanation: 'Above' denotes a position at a higher level or layer than something else.

False
- Explanation: 'Through' is often used to describe movement from one side of an enclosed space to the other.

Short Answer Questions

Example Answer: "The park is located between the museum and the library."
- Explanation: 'Between' is used here to describe a location that is in the middle of two points.

Student's Own Answer
- Expected Explanation: 'Into' indicates movement towards the inside of something, suggesting entering a space, while 'onto' signifies moving on top of a surface.

Advanced Punctuations Answer Key

1. A) She has one goal: to find the treasure.

2. True.

3. "I have everything I need for the trip — including a compass, a map, and a flashlight."

4. B) Twenty-four hours.

5. True.

6. "; for example," or "; however,"

7. A) I need to buy eggs, milk, bread — and don't forget cheese.

8. True.

9. "She knew what her choice would be: pizza."

10. "This is a well-known author."

Complex Sentence Structures Answer Key

Multiple Choice Questions

1. b) Although

   - Explanation: 'Although' is a subordinating conjunction used to introduce a subordinate clause.

2. b) The book that I read was fascinating.

   - Explanation: This sentence uses 'that I read' as a relative clause to give more information about 'the book.'

True or False

3. False

   - Explanation: A complex sentence consists of one independent clause and at least one dependent clause.

4. True

   - Explanation: 'Where' and 'when' can function as relative pronouns to introduce clauses providing information about place and time, respectively.

Short Answer Question

5. Example Answer: "Unless it rains, we will go for a hike tomorrow."

   - Explanation: 'Unless it rains' is a subordinate clause indicating a condition for the action in the independent clause.

Abbreviations ANSWERS

1	O	Ave.	⋯→	Avenue
2	C	Blvd.	⋯→	Boulevard
3	R	Dr.	⋯→	Drive
4	T	Ln.	⋯→	Lane
5	L	Rd.	⋯→	Road
6	H	St.	⋯→	Street
7	D	E	⋯→	east
8	M	N	⋯→	north
9	A	NE	⋯→	northeast
10	U	NW	⋯→	northwest
11	E	S	⋯→	south
12	B	SE	⋯→	southeast
13	V	SW	⋯→	southwest
14	J	W	⋯→	west
15	I	dept.	⋯→	department
16	Q	D.I.Y.	⋯→	Do it yourself
17	S	est.	⋯→	established
18	K	E.T.A.	⋯→	estimated time of arrival
19	P	min.	⋯→	minute or minimum
20	F	misc.	⋯→	miscellaneous
21	N	Mr.	⋯→	Mister
22	G	Mrs.	⋯→	Mistress

Prefixes

A prefix is a part of a word or a word contained within another word. It is added to the beginning of another word to give it a new meaning. Additionally, it can refer to a number that is added at the beginning to indicate the position of anything inside a group.

Rules for adding prefix:

- prefix + root word = new word.

Look at the meaning of the prefix added to the meaning of the root word to get the meaning of the new word.

Meanings for prefixes vary depending on which one is used.

Example:

anti- | opposing, against, the opposite| antibiotic

com- | with, jointly, completely | combat

de- | down, away| decrease|

extra- | outside, beyond | extracurricular

1. **A prefix comes at the _____ of a word.**
   - a. beginning
   - b. end

2. **A prefix changes the meaning of a root word.**
   - a. True
   - b. False

3. **What do you think the prefix re- (redo) means _____?**
   - a. do again
   - b. not - or - opposite

4. **What do you think the prefix dis- (disadvantage) means _____?**
   - a. add; multiply
   - b. away; removal

5. **If you are unable to do something, you are _____.**
   - a. able to do it again
   - b. not able to do it

6. **If you dislike green beans, you _____.**
   - a. really like green beans
   - b. do not like green beans

7. **If you disobey your parents, you _____.**
   - a. obey your parents quickly
   - b. do not obey your parents

8. **My teacher made me ___write name because it was sloppy.**
   - a. un
   - b. re

9. **My friends and I __play our favorite video games over and over again.**
   - a. re
   - b. dis

10. **Kids are __able to drive until they are 16.**
    - a. un
    - b. re

Suffix

A suffix is a letter or group of letters attached to the end of a word in order to alter the meaning or function of the word. As with prefixes, the English language comes with tons of suffixes.

Consider the suffix **-ist**; by adding it to a word, you can modify it to refer to someone who performs or practices something. So, **art** becomes **artist**, a skillful performer of a particular art.

Other Examples:

The suffix **-ish** (Blueish) means relating to or resembling something.

The suffix **-ness** (Happiness) indicates a condition or quality. This suffix changes the word from a verb to a noun.

The suffix **-ship** (internship) position held.

The suffix **-less** (restless) means without something.

1. What is a suffix?

    a. A word beginning that changes the meaning of the word

    b. A word ending that changes the meaning of the word

2. What is the suffix in the word "permission"?

    a. -per

    b. -sion

3. What is the suffix in the word careful?

    a. -care

    b. -ful

4. What is the suffix in the word youngest?

    a. -young

    b. -est

5. What is the suffix in the word harmless?

    a. -less

    b. -arm

6. What is the suffix in the word cuter?

    a. -cute

    b. -er

7. What do you think the suffix -less means?

    a. Meaning: More of

    b. Meaning: Without

8. What do you think the suffix -ward, -wards means? (Towards, afterwards, backwards, inward)

    a. Meaning: Direction

    b. Meaning: Driving something

9. What do you think the suffix -ery means? (bakery, pottery, nursery)

    a. Meaning: an occupation or a way to make a living

    b. Meaning: a business or trade, a behavior, a condition

10. What is the suffix in the word breakable?

    a. -able

    b. -break

Homophones vs Homographs
vs. Homonyms

1. 'there,' 'their,' or 'they're' are examples of _____.
   a. Homophones
   b. Homographs

2. ____ are words that have the same spelling or pronunciation but different meanings.
   a. Homonyms
   b. Hemograms

3. Choose the correct homophone for this sentence: Please don't drop and _____ that bottle of hand sanitizer!
   a. brake
   b. break

4. Homographs are two or more words that have the same spelling but different ____.
   a. ending sounds
   b. meanings

5. Current (A flow of water / Up to date) is both homograph and homophone.
   a. True
   b. False

6. To, two and too are _____.
   a. Homonyms
   b. Homagraphs

7. The candle filled the _____ with a delicious scent.
   a. air
   b. heir

8. Kim drove _____ the tunnel.
   a. threw
   b. through

9. John wants to go to _____ house for dinner, but they don't like her, so _____ going to say no.
   a. there, they're
   b. their, they're

10. We won a $95,000 _____!
    a. check
    b. cheque

11. For example, a pencil is not really made with _____.
    a. led
    b. lead

12. Choose the correct homophone for this sentence: Timmy was standing _____ in line.
    a. fourth
    b. forth

13. Homophones are two words that sound the same but have a different meaning.
    a. True
    b. False

14. The word ring in the following two sentences is considered what? She wore a ruby ring. | We heard the doorbell ring.
    a. hologram
    b. homograph

15. A Homograph is a word that has more than one meaning and doesn't have to sound the same.
    a. True
    b. False

16. Homophones occur when there are multiple ways to spell the same sound.
    a. True
    b. False

17. **Select the correct homophone: I have very little (patience/patients) when students do not follow directions.**

    a. patience

    b. patients

18. **The correct homophone (s) are used in the sentence: Personally, I hate the smell of read meet.**

    a. True

    b. False

19. **The correct homophone(s) is used in the sentence: We saw a herd of cattle in the farmer's field.**

    a. True

    b. False

20. **What is NOT an example of a homograph?**

    a. or, oar

    b. live, live

21. **I love my _____ class.**

    a. dear

    b. deer

22. **We will go _____ after we finish our lesson.**

    a. there

    b. their

23. **Please grab _____ jacket for recess.**

    a. you're

    b. your

24. **There is _____ more water at the concession stand.**

    a. no

    b. know

Collective Noun

A collective noun is a noun that refers to a group of people, animals, or things. They are described as a single entity. Collective nouns are distinct from singular nouns in that singular nouns describe only one person or object.

Many collective nouns are common nouns, but when they are the name of a company or other organization with more than one person, such as Microsoft, they can also be proper nouns.

Find the collective noun in each sentence.

1. Our class visited the natural history museum on a field trip.

   class

2. The bison herd stampeded across the prairie, leaving a massive dust cloud in its wake.

   herd

3. We eagerly awaited the verdict of the jury.

   jury

4. This year's basketball team features three players who stand taller than six feet.

   team

5. At Waterloo, Napoleon's army was finally defeated.

   army

6. The plans for a new park have been approved by the town council.

   council

7. He comes from a large family, as the oldest of eleven children.

   family

8. The rock group has been on tour for several months.

   group

9. When Elvis appeared on stage, the entire audience erupted in applause.

   audience

10. The San Francisco crowd were their usual individualistic selves.

    crowd

11. The crew of sailors boarded the ships.

    crew

12. A mob destroyed the company's new office.

    mob

13. The fleet of ships was waiting at the port.

    fleet

14. It was difficult for the committee to come to a decision.

    committee

Concrete & Abstract Noun

In the English language, both concrete and abstract nouns are essential parts of speech. The primary distinction between concrete and abstract nouns is that concrete nouns refer to people, places, or things that take up physical space, whereas abstract nouns refer to intangible ideas that cannot be physically interacted with.

Words like "luck," "disgust," and "empathy" are examples of abstract nouns. While it is possible to see someone being empathetic, empathy is not a visible or tangible entity. The majority of feelings, emotions, and philosophies can be classified as abstract nouns.

1. FIND THE ABSTRACT NOUN ?

a. KIND

b. BOOK

2. FIND THE CONCRETE NOUNS

a. WINDOW

b. LOVE

3. FIND THE ABSTRACT NOUN: THE KING WAS KNOWN FOR HIS JUSTICE

a. JUSTICE

b. KING

4. WHAT ARE THE 5 CONCRETE NOUNS

a. TASTE, SMELL, WALKING, EYEING, TOUCHING

b. SMELL, TASTE, SIGHT, HEARING, TOUCH

5. WHICH NOUN BELOW IS AN ABSTRACT NOUN?

a. TRAIN

b. LOVE

6. IS THE FOLLOWING NOUN CONCRETE OR ABSTRACT? CUPCAKES

a. ABSTRACT

b. CONCRETE

7. WHAT IS A CONCRETE NOUN?

a. A NOUN THAT YOU CAN EXPERIENCE WITH AT LEAST 1 OF YOUR 5 SENSES.

b. A NOUN THAT YOU CAN'T EXPERIENCE WITH AT LEAST 1 OF YOUR 5 SENSES.

8. WHICH WORD BELOW IS AN ABSTRACT NOUN?

a. BRAVERY

b. FRIEND

9. WHICH WORD BELOW IS NOT A CONCRETE NOUN?

a. HAMBURGER

b. ANGER

10. IS THE WORD THOUGHTFULNESS A CONCRETE OR ABSTRACT NOUN?

a. ABSTRACT

b. CONCRETE

Capitalization Rules Refresher

1. What are the most common pronouns?

   he, she, it, you, her, him, me, I, us, them, they

2. What is a proper noun?

   a name used for an individual person, place, or organization, spelled with initial capital letters

3. Do common nouns name specific persons, places, things, or ideas?

   No: They are not capitalized unless they come at the beginning of a sentence.

4. Always capitalize the first letter in the first word of a sentence?

   Yes

5. Always capitalize the first letter in the first word in a quotation?

   Yes

6. Always capitalize the first letter in the first word of a greeting or closing?

   Yes

7. Always capitalize the first letter in the first and last name of a person?

   Yes

8. Never capitalize the pronoun "I"?   No: I is the only pronoun form that is always capitalized in English.

9. Always capitalize the first letter in the names of: streets, roads, cities, and states?

   Yes

10. Always capitalize the first letter in each part of the name of a specific building or monument: Statue of Liberty, Empire State Building, Pensacola Chamber of Commerce . . .?

    Yes

11. Always capitalize the titles of: video games, stories, movies, and TV shows

    Yes

12. Always capitalize the days of the weeks?

    Yes

13. The names of months should not be capitalized?

    No: Yes, the names of months are always capitalized.

14. Always capitalize major holidays except christmas and thanksgiving?

    No: Christmas and Thanksgiving should be capitalized.

Preposition

1. He pulled **through** his cancer treatment very well.

2. We must pull **together** to make this work.

3. Why don't you put **on** the yellow dress?

4. I have put **off** my holidays until later this year.

5. I don't know how she puts **up** with noisy children all day.

6. The CFS put **out** six fires today.

7. I feel quite run **down** since I got my cold.

8. I might go to Hobart to run **away** from this heat.

9. Coles has run **out** of bread today.

10. You need to set **about** writing your resume.

11. You will never guess who I ran **across** today!

12. I will go to the airport to see **off** my best friend.

13. He set **off** for Paris last Saturday.

14. The little dog was set **upon** by a big dog.

15. Many students want to set **up** their own business.

Acronym

A common way to make an acronym is to use the first letter of each word in a phrase to make a word that can be spoken. This is a great way to make a longer, more complicated phrase easier to say and shorter.

Carefully choose the acronym for each word or phrase.

1. Also Known As
   a. AKA
   b. KAA

2. Central Standard Time
   a. CST
   b. TCS

3. Doing Business As
   a. DBA
   b. ASDOING

4. Do Not Disturb
   a. NOTDN
   b. DND

5. Electronic Data Systems
   a. SDE
   b. EDS

6. End of Day
   a. EOD
   b. ENDDAY

7. Eastern Standard Time
   a. EST
   b. TSE

8. Estimated Time of Arrival
   a. ET
   b. ETA

9. Human Resources
   a. HRS
   b. HR

10. Masters of Business Administration
   a. MOBA
   b. MBA

11. MST - Mountain Standard Time
   a. MST
   b. MSTS

12. Overtime
   a. OTIME
   b. OT

13. Point Of Service
   a. POS
   b. POOS

14. Pacific Standard Time
   a. PST
   b. PSTE

15. Anti-lock Braking System
   a. LOCKBS
   b. ABS

16. Attention Deficit Disorder
   a. ADD
   b. ATTDD

17. Attention Deficit Hyperactivity Disorder

    a. ADHP

    b. ADHD

18. Acquired Immune Deficiency Syndrome

    a. ACQIMDEF

    b. AIDS

19. Centers for Disease Control and Prevention

    a. CDC

    b. CDCP

20. Dead On Arrival

    a. DONA

    b. DOA

21. Date Of Birth

    a. DOB

    b. DOFB

22. Do It Yourself

    a. DIY

    b. DIYO

23. Frequently Asked Questions

    a. FAQA

    b. FAQ

24. Graphics Interchange Format

    a. GIF

    b. GIFF

25. Human Immunodeficiency Virus

    a. HIV

    b. HIMMV

26. Medical Doctor

    a. MD

    b. MED

27. Over The Counter

    a. OTC

    b. OTHEC

28. Pay Per View

    a. PPV

    b. PAYPPV

29. Sound Navigation And Ranging

    a. SONAR

    b. SONAVR

30. Sports Utility Vehicle

    a. SPOUV

    b. SUV

Adjectives to Describe People

Adjectives are descriptive or modifying words for nouns or pronouns. For instance, adjectives such as red, quick, happy, and annoying exist to describe things—a red hat, a speedy rabbit, a cheerful duck, and an obnoxious individual.

Unscramble the adjectives to describe people.

polite	friendly	clever	outgoing	good looking	handsome
cute	fat	tall	smart	young	pretty
attractive	rude	easygoing	funny	confident	tidy
old	beautiful	generous	ugly		

1. ulbuefita   b e a u t i f u l

2. trpyet   p r e t t y

3. etuc   c u t e

4. luyg   u g l y

5. ugnyo   y o u n g

6. tleipo   p o l i t e

7. nnufy   f u n n y

8. riledfny   f r i e n d l y

9. ohemndsa   h a n d s o m e

10. rdue   r u d e

11. dol   o l d

12. aft   f a t

13. mrtas   s m a r t

14. idty   t i d y

15. yogsgeain   e a s y g o i n g

16. cleerv   c l e v e r

17. neeugrso   g e n e r o u s

18. fnitnedoc   c o n f i d e n t

19. tngioogu   o u t g o i n g

20. dgoo oinogkl   g o o d   l o o k i n g

21. vractatite   a t t r a c t i v e

22. tlla   t a l l

Contractions Multiple Choice

A *contraction* is a way of making two words into one. Circle the correct answer.

1. aren't
    a. are not
    b. not are
    c. arenot

2. can't
    a. cants
    b. cannot
    c. cant

3. couldn't
    a. couldnt
    b. couldnts
    c. could not

4. didn't
    a. didn'ts
    b. did nots
    c. did not

5. don't
    a.
    b. do not

6. hadn't
    a. had not
    b. had nots
    c. hadn'ts

7. hasn't
    a. has nots
    b. has not
    c. hasnot

8. haven't
    a. have nots
    b. haven'ts
    c. have not

9. I'm
    a. I am
    b. I'ms
    c. I'am

10. I've
    a. I have
    b. I'ves
    c. I'have

11. isn't
    a. isn'ts
    b. is not
    c. is'not

12. let's
    a. lets
    b. let'us
    c. let us

13. mightn't
    a. mightnt
    b. might not
    c. might'not

14. mustn't
    a. mustnt
    b. must'not
    c. must not

Demonstrative Pronoun

This, That, These, and Those

Words that point to specific things are known as demonstrative pronouns. "This is a pencil," for example.

These pronouns indicate the relationship between the speaker and the object:

- this / these: an object or objects in close proximity to the person speaking (often within touching distance)
- that / those: an object or objects distant from the person speaking (often out of touching distance)
- that over there / those over there: object or objects located a long distance away from the person

1. _____ orange I'm eating is delicious.
   - a. These
   - b. [This]
   - c. That

2. It is better than _____ apples from last week.
   - a. that
   - b. these
   - c. [those]

3. Astronauts don't get fresh fruit like _____ peaches we are eating.
   - a. this
   - b. [these]
   - c. that

4. _____ meals they take into space are freeze-dried.
   - a. [Those]
   - b. That
   - c. This

5. _____ fact means they must add water to them.
   - a. These
   - b. This here
   - c. [That]

6. _____ granola bars are tasty too.
   - a. [These]
   - b. Them
   - c. This here

7. Don't sign me up for _____ next shuttle flight.
   - a. these here
   - b. [that]
   - c. that there

8. _____ book is so heavy I can hardly lift it.
   - a. Those
   - b. This here
   - c. [This]

9. Some believed _____ dream could be a reality.
   - a. that there
   - b. these
   - c. [that]

10. _____ change is due to our astronauts.
    - a. [This]
    - b. That there
    - c. These here

Refresher: Simple, Compound & Complex

1. 'Darkness cannot drive out darkness; only light can do that.' - Martin Luther King Jr.

   a. Compound sentence
   b. Complex sentence
   c. Dependent clause

2. 'Beauty is in the heart of the beholder.' - H.G. Wells

   a. Dependent clause
   b. Independent clause
   c. Simple sentence

3. Their robot can follow a simple path through a maze.

   a. compound sentence
   b. simple sentence
   c. complex sentence

4. Kristina was late because she the traffic was terrible.

   a. compound sentence
   b. complex sentence
   c. simple sentence

5. He won the prize, but he was not happy.

   a. complex sentence
   b. compound sentence
   c. simple sentence

6. 'Silence is golden when you can't think of a good answer.' - Muhammad Ali

   a. Complex sentence
   b. Dependent clause
   c. Independent clause

7. Although it was cold, we played the match.

   a. Complex sentence
   b. Independent clause
   c. Dependent clause

8. 'People won't have time for you if you are always angry or complaining.' - Stephen Hawking

   a. Simple sentence
   b. Independent clause
   c. Complex sentence

Tenses

borrowed	went	eat	play	go	giving
read	give	gave	will eat	yelled	seeing
will have	had	reading	will go	do	will borrow
playing	doing	yelling	did	will yell	will do
will give	fight	borrow	yell	will fight	will play
borrowing	played	fighting	read	have	will see
going	see	will read	fought	eating	ate
saw	having				

Simple Present (11)	Present Progressive (IS/ARE +) (11)	Past (11)	Future (11)
play	playing	played	will play
go	going	went	will go
read	reading	read	will read
borrow	borrowing	borrowed	will borrow
eat	eating	ate	will eat
have	having	had	will have
see	seeing	saw	will see
fight	fighting	fought	will fight
do	doing	did	will do
give	giving	gave	will give
yell	yelling	yelled	will yell

Fictional vs. Fictitious vs. Fictive

Fictional is invented as part of a work of fiction

SYNONYMS:
Fabricated
Imaginary

Fictitious is created, taken, or assumed for the sake of concealment; not genuine; false

SYNONYMS:
Bogus
Counterfeit

Fictive - fictitious; imaginary. pertaining to the creation of fiction
- is capable of imaginative creation.

SYNONYMS:

Make-believe
Fabricated

1. He dismissed recent rumors about his private life as _____.
   a. fictitious
   b. fictional
   c. fictive

2. I have the impression that this _____ marriage of ours is like a ghost in a play.
   a. fictional
   b. fictitious
   c. fictive

3. The setting is a _____ island in the Chesapeake River.
   a. fictitious
   b. fictional
   c. fictive

4. The writer has _____ talent.
   a. fictitious
   b. fictional
   c. fictive

5. Almost all _____ detectives are unreal.
   a. fictitious
   b. fictional
   c. fictive

6. The names of the shops are entirely _____.
   a. fictive
   b. fictional
   c. fictitious

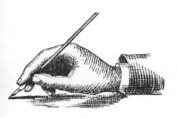

Fill-in The Appositive

Appositives are words or phrases that come before or after other nouns or pronouns to describe them further. The appositives should give the reader additional information about the nouns and pronouns in the sentences. Keep in mind that an appositive can be a single word or a group of words.

Appositives can be either essential or non-essential. If the appositive is required for the sentence to make sense, it is essential. This means it cannot be omitted. If the appositive is not required for the sentence's meaning and could be excluded, it is nonessential.

Commas should be used to separate non-essential appositives from the sentence. Commas are not used to separate essential appositives.

Examples:

Jane, my younger sister, is 27 years old. (Jane renames her younger sister)

My mother, who works as a nurse, has a red automobile. (A nurse renames mother, but this isn't necessary for the meaning of the line.)

Kevin is the name of the young artist that created this painting. (Who painted this image renames boy, which is crucial to the sentence's meaning.)

An insect, a ladybug, has just landed on the rose bush.

| meadowlark | fiancé | cousin | valedictorian | Jones |
| champion | governor | movie | capital | |

1. My uncle, the former **governor** of Maine, loves ice cream

2. Sally's **fiancé** Gerald works at Walmart

3. Providence, the **capital** of RI, is a great city

4. We saw the state bird, the **meadowlark** , at the park

5. My youngest **cousin** Caroline goes to Princeton University

6. Muhammad Ali, the three time heavy weight **champion** of the world won a gold medal in 1960

7. Sally Smith, the **valedictorian** , gave a wonderful speech at graduation

8. The vice principal, Mr. **Jones** , suspended my brother

9. My favorite **movie** , "Stand and Deliver" always makes me cry.

Informational Text

1. **Identify the main idea: "You wouldn't use a nail file to peel carrots. You can't tune an engine with a cheese grater, either. So why would you buy a wrench to do the job of a screwdriver?"**
   a. Always use the right tool.
   b. Wrench and screwdrivers are basically the same.
   c. Use nail file for your fingernails.

2. **Autobiographies are written in which point of view?**
   a. second
   b. third
   c. first

3. **Differentiate between a plot and a theme.**
   a. A plot is the ending in a story, a theme conveys the message in first person
   b. A theme is a collection of the main idea, while a plot conveys the point of the ending
   c. A plot is more of what happens in a story, whereas a theme conveys the message of the story

4. **Which is not an article in a reference book?**
   a. thesaurus entry for the word army
   b. encyclopedia article on World War II
   c. a review of a novel

5. **When creating summaries, it's important to _____.**
   a. tell the ending of the story
   b. Write down the main points in your own words
   c. Use the first person exact words

6. **Which type of literary nonfiction is not meant to be published or shared?**
   a. biography
   b. diary
   c. memoir

7. **Which of the following should you do as you read an informational text?**
   a. Take notes
   b. find clue words and text
   c. read as quickly as possible

8. **What makes a speech different from an article?**
   a. speeches are meant to be spoken aloud to an audience
   b. speeches do not inform about a topic
   c. articles can persuade a reader

9. **Which type of literary nonfiction is a short piece on a single topic?**
   a. essay
   b. letter
   c. memoir

10. **Procedural writing example:**
    a. letter to the editor, blog entry
    b. textbook, travel brochure
    c. cookbooks, how-to articles, instruction manuals

Homophones - Words that are pronounced the same but they have different meanings.

Match the homophones.

1	K	oar	⋯➤	or
2	P	pair	⋯➤	pear
3	Q	plain	⋯➤	plane
4	B	pray	⋯➤	prey
5	L	profit	⋯➤	prophet
6	F	right	⋯➤	write
7	I	sail	⋯➤	sale
8	J	seam	⋯➤	seem
9	H	sow	⋯➤	sight
10	C	sole	⋯➤	soul
11	G	son	⋯➤	sun
12	D	stationary	⋯➤	stationery
13	O	suite	⋯➤	sweet
14	A	their	⋯➤	there
15	N	two	⋯➤	toe
16	M	wait	⋯➤	weight
17	E	weak	⋯➤	week

Identify The Various Parts of Grammar

Across

1. the first word in a noun group
2. a word used to describe a noun
3. the first part of a sentence is called the ....
7. this tells us how many of a noun (some / ten / a few)
10. a sentence that uses a conjunction to join two independent clauses
11. a sentence with a dependent clause and one or more independent clauses
12. one conjunction is ....
15. a clause beginning with if / when / because is called ....
18. the last part of a sentence is called ....
19. a phrase beginning with a preposition is called ....

Down

3. What type of sentence is one independent clause
4. an independent clause can only have one ....
5. The last word of a noun group
6. a / an / the are called
8. this / that / these / those are called ....
9. tells us who owns the noun
13. we change the verb to make past ....
14. a story written or spoken in past tense
16. a clause that contains the full meaning is called ....
20. the conjunctions so and because give us a result and ....

ADJECTIVE   INDEPENDENT
COMPLEX   TENSE   DEPENDENT
BECAUSE   VERB
POSSESSIVE   QUANTIFIER
COMPOUND   SIMPLE
PREPOSITIONAL   RECOUNT
DETERMINER   ARTICLE
OBJECT   REASON   SUBJECT
DEMONSTRATIVE   NOUN

Mood and Modality in Verbs Answer Key

Multiple Choice Answers

1. c) Subjunctive - The verb "speak" is used in a subjunctive mood to express a suggestion.

2. b) Imperative - This sentence gives a command.

True or False Answers

1. False - The sentence uses the subjunctive mood ("be informed" indicates necessity).

2. False - The sentence is indicative, stating a fact about his daily routine.

Short Answer Examples

1. Example: "If I were president, I would change the law." (Subjunctive expresses a hypothetical situation)

2. The imperative mood typically makes a sentence direct and commanding. It's often used in giving orders, making requests, or offering advice.

Nouns, Adverbs, and Verbs Review Answer Key

1. Cat

2. Abstract noun

3. Car

4. Amazon River

5. Example: "Freedom is essential for happiness."

6. Friend, gift

7. Teacher, book, class

8. Abstract noun

9. Example: "The light from the lamp was bright."

10. Elephant

Adverbs Answers

1. Quickly

2. Example: "The cat moved silently through the house."

3. Softly

4. Happily

5. How the dog barked (loudly)

6. Degree

7. Example: "I went to the cinema yesterday."

8. Abundantly

9. Incredibly

10. Example: "He often goes for a walk in the park."

Verbs Answers

1. Flies

2. Example: "We love to dance at parties."

3. Sing

4. Sing

5. Example: "I think you are right."

6. Rises

7. Walked, bought

8. State of being verb

9. Example: "I study hard for my exams."

10. Have finished

Possessive nouns, Pronouns, Plural Nouns Review Answer Key

Possessive Nouns

1. cyclist's

2. dog's

3. The man's hat was left on the table.

4. Sarah's

5. The children's playground is newly renovated.

Pronouns

1. they

2. it

3. mine

4. Possessive

5. They played in the park, and they had a lot of fun.

Plural Nouns

1. Foxes

2. books

3. The children played in the yard.

4. geese

5. The women are walking their dogs.

Reading Comprehension
Alphabetical Order

1. Which word follows "engage" in the dictionary?

    a. encounter

    b. erase

    c. energy

    d. emigrant

2. Which word would follow "honor" in the dictionary?

    a. hiccup

    b. hesitate

    c. humble

    d. hideout

3. Which word would follow "linoleum" in the dictionary?

    a. literature

    b. lightning

    c. lilac

    d. liberty

4. Which word would follow "minute" in the dictionary?

    a. method

    b. mimic

    c. misery

    d. minister

5. Which word would follow "pleasure" in the dicitonary?

    a. pliers

    b. photo

    c. platinum

    d. place

6. What word follows "proceed" in the dictionary?

    a. product

    b. program

    c. probable

    d. priority

7. What word follow "respiration" in the dictionary?

    a. resound

    b. resign

    c. resort

    d. respond

8. What word follows "sneeze" in the dictionary?

    a. slumber

    b. snarl

    c. snatch

    d. snorkel

9. What word follows "territory" in the dictionary?

    a. textile

    b. terrific

    c. telescope

    d. tarnish

10. What word follows "curtain" in the dictionary?

    a. crumble

    b. curse

    c. cube

    d. customer

Root Words, Prefixes, and Suffixes **Answer Key:**

1. A) Not

   Explanation: "Un-" is a prefix that means "not," making "unbelievable" mean "not believable."

2. False

   Explanation: "Careless" means "without care," not "full of care." The suffix "-less" means "without."

3. "Hopefulness"

   Explanation: Adding the suffix "-fulness" to "hope" forms "hopefulness," meaning the state of having hope.

4. Root word: "Agree"

   Explanation: The prefix "dis-" means "not" and the suffix "-ment" turns it into a noun, so "disagreement" means "the state of not agreeing."

5. A-2, B-3, C-1, D-4

   Explanation: "Pre-" means "before," "-able" means "capable of," "re-" means "again," and "-ness" refers to "state of."

Test Your Knowledge Answer Key

Part 1: Parts of Speech

1. False. A verb is a word that describes an action or a state of being. A noun is a person, place, thing, or idea.
2. C. Blue - An adjective is a word that describes or modifies a noun.
3. Slept - This is the action the cat is performing.

Part 2: Verb Tenses

4. False. The past perfect tense describes an action that has happened before another action in the past.
5. Is running - The present progressive tense indicates an ongoing action happening right now.
6. Had - The correct form is "had already started," using the past perfect tense to show the movie starting happened before the arrival at the cinema.

Part 3: Sentence Structure

7. False. A compound sentence contains two or more independent clauses, and may be joined by a coordinating conjunction (for, and, nor, but, or, yet, so). A complex sentence contains one independent clause and one or more dependent clauses.
8. Flowers - Even though "flowers" comes after "bloom," it's what's doing the blooming, so it's the subject.
9. Answers may vary. Example: "Although I studied hard, I didn't do well on the test."

Part 4: Punctuation

10. True. A semicolon can be used to connect two closely related independent clauses that could stand alone as separate sentences if needed.
11. B. "Let's eat, grandma!" - The comma is necessary to clearly separate the clauses and avoid confusion.
12. Corrected sentence: "She said, 'I'm sorry for your loss.'" - When dialogue is reported, it should be enclosed in quotation marks, with a comma indicating the pause before the spoken words.

This, That, These, and Those

This, that, these and those are demonstratives. We use this, that, these, and those to point to people and things. This and that are singular. These and those are plural.

1. _____ orange I'm eating is delicious.
- a. This
- b. These
- c. Those
- d. That

2. It is better than _____ apples from last week.
- a. that
- b. those
- c. these
- d. this

3. Let's exchange _____ bread for these crackers.
- a. those
- b. this
- c. these
- d. that

4. Let's try some of _____ freeze-dried steak.
- a. this
- b. this here
- c. them
- d. those there

5. Is _____ water boiling yet?
- a. these here
- b. that
- c. that there
- d. this here

6. _____ granola bars are tasty too.
- a. These
- b. This here
- c. Them
- d. These here

7. _____ mountains don't look that far away.
- a. This
- b. Those
- c. These
- d. That

8. I like _____ pictures better than those.
- a. this
- b. that
- c. those
- d. these

9. _____ car at the far end of the lot is mine.
- a. That
- b. This
- c. These
- d. Those

10. I like the feel of _____ fabric.
- a. those
- b. this here
- c. that there
- d. this

11. In _____ early days, space travel was a dream.
- a. that
- b. them
- c. those
- d. this

12. _____ days, we believe humans will go to Mars.
- a. These
- b. This
- c. Those
- d. That

Understanding Conjunctions Answer Key

Multiple Choice Answers:

1. B) And

2. B) Subordinating

3. B) Not only...but also

True or False Answers:

1. True. "Yet" is used to introduce a contrasting idea.

2. True. Subordinating conjunctions can start a sentence, especially in complex sentences.

3. False. "Whether...or" is a correlative conjunction.

Short Answer Sample Answers:

1. Example: "I wanted to go for a walk, but it was raining."

2. Coordinating conjunctions connect words, phrases, or clauses of equal grammatical rank. Subordinating conjunctions connect a dependent clause to an independent clause, indicating a relationship like cause and effect, time, or condition.

3. Example: "Neither the cold weather nor the heavy traffic could dampen her spirits."

No answers for the extra credit writing exercise.

Alphabetize and Define

meter	1. alliteration
irony	2. connotation
personification	3. denotation
denotation	4. imagery
onomatopoeia	5. irony
alliteration	6. metaphor
rhyme	7. meter
metaphor	8. onomatopoeia
theme	9. personification
symbolism	10. repetition
repetition	11. rhyme
simile	12. simile
stanza	13. stanza
connotation	14. symbolism
imagery	15. theme

After putting the words in alphabetical order, choose 5 and write a definition in the space provided.

[Student worksheet has a 5 line writing exercise here.]

Apostrophe

1. Where should the apostrophe go in didnt?
   a. didn't
   b. did'nt

2. How do you make the contraction for was not?
   a. was'nt
   b. wasn't

3. How do you make Jimmy possessive?
   a. Jimmy's
   b. Jimmys

4. Where should the apostrophe go in shouldnt?
   a. should'nt
   b. shouldn't

5. How do you make the contraction for she would?
   a. she'd
   b. sh'ed

6. What is the correct use of the apostrophe?
   a. brother's toys
   b. brother'is toys

7. Which of the following is the correct way to show possession with a plural noun ending in 's'?
   a. Add an apostrophe at the end.
   b. No apostrophe is required.

8. How would you express the plural possessive of the word 'child'?
   a. Child's
   b. Children's

9. What is the proper way to contract the possessive form of 'it'?
   a. Its
   b. It's

10. The _____ awfully good today.
   a. weather
   b. weather's

11. Adam believes _____ going to snow later.
   a. it's
   b. its

12. The dog was wagging _____ tail excitedly.
   a. its
   b. it's

13. Where did you leave _____ book?
   a. your
   b. you're

14. _____ going to Ms. Katy's room.
   a. Wer'e
   b. We're

15. Bobby always kicks _____ dolls around.
   a. Kim and Sandy's
   b. Jennifer and Katie

16. _____ not allowed to listen to music while they read.
   a. They're
   b. Their're

Grammar Review

1. His father is the coach of the team.

   a. his, father, team

   b. his, father, coach

   c. father, coach, team

2. David is driving to the beach.

   a. David, driving, beach

   b. David, driving

   c. David, beach

3. What are the PROPER nouns in the following sentence? My **grandparents live in Florida.**

   a. grandparents, Flordia

   b. Flordia

   c. My, grandparents

4. What are all the COMMON nouns in the following sentence? I have two dogs and one cat.

   a. cat, one

   b. dogs, cat

   c. I, dogs

5. Which sentence contains only one common noun and one proper noun?

   a. These potatoes are from Idaho.

   b. Casey is a talented singer and dancer.

   c. I live near the border of Nevada and Utah.

6. Which sentence contains the correct form of a plural noun?

   a. The wolves chase a frightened rabbit.

   b. The wolfes chase a frightened rabbit.

   c. The wolfs chase a frightened rabbit.

7. Which sentence contains one singular noun and one plural noun?

   a. The musician tunes her instrument.

   b. The conductor welcomes each musician.

   c. The singers walk across the stage.

8. Identify the collective noun in the following sentence.
Derek is the lead singer in a band.

   a. singer

   b. band

   c. lead

9. Which sentence contains the correct form of a singular possessive noun?

   a. The boxs' lid is torn.

   b. The box's lid is torn.

   c. The boxes' lid is torn.

10. Which sentence contains one concrete noun and on abstract noun?

   a. John feels anxiety about meeting new people.

   b. The young boy plays with trains.

   c. The sand feels warm between my toes.

11. Identify the simple subject in the following sentence. The **children are playing tag.**

   a. tag

   b. children

   c. The children

12. Identify the simple subject in the following sentence. This computer belongs to my father.

   a. computer

   b. This computer

   c. father

13. **Which sentence has an object of a preposition?**

   a. Several passengers missed the flight.

   b. Seattle is a city in Washington.

   c. The boys are racing remote-controlled cars.

14. **Identify the object of preposition in the following sentence.**
   The are playing a game of cards.

   a. cards

   b. game

   c. of cards

15. **Identify the subject complement in the following sentence.**
   Mr. Smith is a talented poet.

   a. poet

   b. talented

   c. Mr. Smith

16. **Identify the subject complement in the following sentence.**
   Tulips and daisies are my favorite flowers.

   a. my

   b. flowers

   c. favorite

17. **Identify the direct object in the following sentence.** **Tyler delivers newspapers each morning.**

   a. newspapers

   b. morning

   c. each

18. **Identify the direct object in the following sentence.** **We will paint the bathroom beige.**

   a. bathroom

   b. paint

   c. beige

19. **Identify the indirect object in the following sentence.** **Mr. Jackson gave the students their grades.**

   a. grades

   b. students

   c. their

20. **Identify the indirect object in the following sentence.** **Mrs. Parker bought her husband a new tie.**

   a. new tie

   b. husband

   c. tie

21. **In which sentence is paint used as a noun?**

   a. These artists paint the most amazing murals.

   b. We need two cans of brown paint.

   c. Let's paint the bedroom light green.

22. **In which sentence is sign used as a verb?**

   a. I saw it as a sign of good luck.

   b. Joelle is learning sign language.

   c. Did you sign the letter at the bottom?

23. **In which sentence is file used as an adjective?**

   a. This file contains the detective's notes.

   b. Put these papers in a file folder.

   c. I use a file to smooth the edges of my nails.

24. **Identify the direct address in the following sentence.** **This is your baseball bat, Kenny.**

   a. Kenny

   b. baseball

   c. bat

25. **Identify the direct address in the following sentence.**
    Hector, did you buy more milk?

    a. [Hector]
    b. you
    c. milk

26. **Objects of the preposition. Lee cried during the movie.**

    a. Lee
    b. [movie]
    c. cried

27. **Objects of the preposition. The phone is on the table.**

    a. [table]
    b. phone
    c. none

28. **Direct Objects: Every actor played his part.**

    a. [his part]
    b. actor
    c. played

29. **Direct Objects: The crowd will cheer the President.**

    a. [the President]
    b. cheer
    c. crowd

30. **Examples of concrete nouns are:**

    a. [flower, music, bear, pie,]
    b. love, cars, them, went
    c. me, I, she, they

31. **Direct Address: Well certainly, Mother, I remember what you said.**

    a. you
    b. [Mother]
    c. certainly

32. **Direct Address: I heard exactly what you said, Pam.**

    a. [Pam]
    b. none
    c. you

33. **Collective Noun: A choir of singers**

    a. [choir]
    b. sing
    c. singers

34. **Collective Noun: A litter of puppies**

    a. [litter]
    b. puppies
    c. puppy

End of the Year Evaluation

Name: _____

Grade/Level: _____ Date: _____

Subjects Studied: _____

_____

_____

Goals Accomplished: _____

_____

_____

_____

Most Improved Areas: _____

_____

_____

_____

Areas of Improvement: _____

_____

_____

Main Curriculum Evaluation	Satisfied		A= Above Standards	Final Grades
_____	Yes	No	S= Meets Standards	
			N= Needs Improvement	_____
_____	Yes	No	98-100 A+	
			93-97 A	_____
_____	Yes	No	90-92 A	
			88-89 B+	_____
_____	Yes	No	83-87 B	
			80-82 B	_____
_____	Yes	No	78-79 C+	
			73-77 C	_____
_____	Yes	No	70-72 C	
			68-69 D+	_____
			62-67 D	
			60-62 D	
			59 & Below F	

Most Enjoyed: _____

_____

Least Enjoyed: _____

_____

GRADES TRACKER

Week	Monday	Tuesday	Wednesday	Thursday	Friday
1					
2					
3					
4					
5					
6					
7					
8					
9					
10					
11					
12					
13					
14					
15					
16					
17					
18					

Notes

Made in the USA
Las Vegas, NV
05 April 2024